Training
Ain't
Performance

- Why training doesn't guarantee job performance

- What it takes to drive performance success

- How to achieve remarkable performance results everyone values

**ASTD Press** **ISPI**
Improving Performance
Since 1962

Harold D. Stolovitch
Erica J. Keeps

1958-62220

ASTD Press is an internationally renowned source of insightful and practical information on workplace learning and performance topics, including training basics, evaluation and return-on-investment (ROI), instructional systems development (ISD), e-learning, leadership, and career development.

Ordering information: Books published by ASTD Press can be purchased by visiting our Website at store.astd.org or by calling 800.628.2783 or 703.683.8100.

Library of Congress Catalog Card Number: 2004101572

ISBN: 1-56286-367-3

Acquisitions and Development Editor: Mark Morrow
Copyeditor: Nancy Berg
Interior Design and Production: Kathleen Schaner
Cover Design: Charlene Osman
Cover Illustration: Mark Shaver

Printed by Victor Graphics, Inc., Baltimore, Maryland. www.victorgraphics.com

Contents

Preface

What delight and astonishment we felt when we discovered how well our previous volume, *Telling Ain't Training*, had been received! It was a joy pulling together our many years of practice and research in the field of learning and presenting it in a fun, interactive manner, while still preserving the integrity of what makes excellent "training" work. However, we were also left with a nagging sense that we had not recounted the entire tale. Sure, telling ain't training. More important, however, training ain't performance—and performance, after all, is why organizations spend enormous sums of money (more than $60 billion annually in the United States) and devote such energy and resources to training their personnel.

In simple terms, workplace organizations—companies, hospitals, the military, government, social agencies, and even volunteer groups—require that people be able to do something of value. If the organizations are not getting the desired results, they either have to find people who can meet the need or else do something with the people they have to get them to perform. In the latter case, the usual default intervention is training. In *Telling Ain't Training*, we focused on how to obtain the best and the most from your training efforts.

But what if training is not the answer or is not enough? Then what? This is the perfect question to launch this book. What you will discover in the ensuing pages is that the path to successful performance for your organization and its people does not always lead to training. In fact, the path may head off in several other directions.

Our professional lives have been devoted to helping people perform in ways that both they and their organizations value. We want to engage you in this wonderful cause. Take the journey with us through this book. We promise you an active and interactive ride. Enjoy . . . and learn!

Before we begin, there are two important points. As you embark upon the *Training Ain't Performance* adventure, you will come across three signposts or icons.

 This icon signals an important fact. Stop for a moment to investigate and reflect.

This icon identifies key points for using the information we've supplied. These are worth noting.

 This icon accompanies a review of the major take-away knowledge in each chapter. Spend a moment here to collect your thoughts before moving on.

The second point that is important to anyone concerned about performance is that a book such as this one requires the support and encouragement of many individuals to bring it to life. Our profound thanks go out to Mark Morrow, acquisitions editor of the American Society for Training & Development, who enthusiastically encouraged us to produce this volume. Mark makes writing a great pleasure through his constant assistance and facilitation.

From manuscript to published work requires the skillful editing and guidance of a devoted and sensitive editor. Our heartfelt appreciation and thanks to Nancy Berg for making what we had to say cleaner, crisper, and more communicably sound.

In our work, nothing goes out the door until professionals whom we respect read, review, and give sage feedback and advice on the manuscripts we produce. This is an arduous task of professional courtesy. Thank you Daniel Blair, Linda Kemp, and Miki Lane for taking time from your busy schedules to provide such rich and useful content suggestions.

Thank you also Jennifer Papineau, our graphic and technical support advisor, for all the counsel you have provided from start to finish. We admire your ideas and results.

As always, we are stymied by what to say by way of thanks to Samantha Greenhill, who works with us every day to transform our rough words and edges into far more presentable forms. Ever patient and present, Sam is truly a collaborator in the creation of this book. Thanks from the bottom of our hearts.

We dedicate this book to Ellen Vorzimer—Aunt Ellen—who is a model of peak performance in action.

Finally, as we have always done in our partnership as authors, we thank one another for the support, encouragement, and understanding each has given the other throughout the writing of this volume. As a professional couple constantly working together, bringing this book to fruition has been a true labor of love.

Harold D. Stolovitch
Erica J. Keeps
Los Angeles
May 2004

Chapter 1

Show Me the Money!

Show Me the Money! Case Study

Melvyn is a 28-year-old college graduate who works as a loan officer at your bank. Let's observe Melvyn in action. It's 8:00 a.m., the official start of the workday, and there he is, already 30 minutes into his duties, reviewing files, an activity schedule, and a list of clients and payments. Melvyn is neatly groomed, dressed in shirt and tie, and appears to be both professionally engaged and on top of things. His desk is as neat as his personal appearance.

It's now 8:15 a.m. and whom do we see entering the adjoining office? Marna. Her hair is windblown as she breezes in wearing a work shirt and jeans. Her office is filled with odds and ends, and her desk is covered with publications and file folders. Marna is 27 and a lender too. Like Melvyn, she is responsible for identifying loan clients in the commercial sector and making productive, profitable loans. That's what your bank is all about! Melvyn and Marna have been through extensive lending training, and each has been in his or her position for nine months. They have taken follow-up courses. Both were tops in their training programs and fared well on the certification exams. The two of them were identified early on as high achievers.

As you observe them now, you note the following characteristics:

Melvyn	Marna
• Neat, polite, energetic, prudent • Excellent oral and written communication skills • Always punctual at the office • Always reports in on time • Always available and accessible at the bank • Not one default in his loan portfolio • Serious, focused, motivated • Eager to please	• Casual dresser, crisp, always on the move, risk-taker • Terse and telegraphic in oral and written communications; a bullet-point person • Frequently late arriving at the office • Sometimes reports late • Not often available; frequently out of the bank • Several loan defaults or "in-jeopardy" cases • Smiley, curious, task-focused • Not a "political" player; forceful

So, it's decision time for you as their manager. Which one do you think is the better performer? Check your choice below.

- ☐ **Melvyn**
- ☐ **Marna**
- ☐ **I don't know**

Melvyn looks very good. His behaviors appear to be positive. No loan defaults is certainly a plus. He performed beautifully in his training. Seems to be a good choice.

Marna's behaviors are not looking good. Writes and speaks in a pretty abbreviated manner, although she is nice to be with and always seems interested in new ideas. She's often late to work and leaves early. A bit messy, too. Hmmm?

"I don't know" sounds like a cop-out. Nevertheless, this may be your wisest choice. At the moment, do you have all the facts about their performance with respect to the bank's goals? Please give us your full attention as we investigate more deeply.

Facts:

- ◆ Both performed well in the training. Both "know the job."
- ◆ Melvyn has no loan defaults. He also has very few loans out because he has been extra careful in risking the bank's funds. He waits for loan applications to come in, investigates them very carefully, and only proposes loans where there is sound, experienced management; sufficient collateral; an established market; and a strong track record of loan repayment.
- ◆ Marna has pushed through a few loans that have defaulted. However, her portfolio of loans is almost four times greater than Melvyn's. She is out in the marketplace daily, scouting import-export meetings, high-tech fairs, and biotech conferences, among other events. She visits new-age farms, factories, and freight yards, often at the crack of dawn when

many of her prospects have time for an early morning coffee and chat. Her contribution to bank revenues is three times that of Melvyn's contribution, despite the defaults.

◆ Melvyn's office is neat and orderly, and his files are up-to-date.

◆ Marna's office is jammed with brochures, reports, conference programs, and market research data files. Some of her administrative work is behind schedule.

◆ Melvyn is available to the bank.

◆ Marna is available to customers.

Shall we try again? Which one do you think is the better performer? Check your choice below.

☐ **Melvyn**
☐ **Marna**
☐ **I don't know**

By now, you have probably made up your mind. Given the new facts, you more than likely chose Marna. Rightly so.

Both went through extensive training and fared similarly on the exams. However, each then selected a different path to follow. The goal of the bank is to increase its revenues and profits, and it is looking for "new-economy loans" involving fresh entrepreneurial talent with bold, new ideas. These loans potentially provide higher yields than solid, traditional company loans. With this in mind, who is "performing better"?

What This Book Is About

We assume that you're getting the message. Melvyn and Marna are equally bright and motivated and are beneficiaries of the same training. Yet they have ended up performing differently. Training ain't performance.

In the workplace, despite the explicit emphasis on "bottom-line results," there is still an enormous confusion between behaviors—activities—and valued accomplishments, between knowing and achieving, and between training and performance. This book is aimed at untangling some of the myths, fallacies, and confusions that organizations often propagate and that are counterproductive to true, valued performance. So here is what *Training Ain't Performance* provides for you:

◆ *A well-documented and substantial portrait of what performance is and is not in the world of work.* Through examples, exercises, anecdotes, and questions, we offer you a clear explanation of what desired workplace performance is and how you can obtain it. We have spent most of our careers researching and practicing human performance improvement. In this book, we share with you our findings and experiences as well as those of others. However, we do this in a nonacademic way. The goal is for you to be able to define performance and design the appropriate means for you and your organization or clients to achieve it.

- *A simple, friendly, easy-to-read style of writing.* You have already experienced this with Melvyn and Marna. We have made every effort to communicate and interact with you as if we were engaged in a conversation. However, please don't let the style fool you. Everything we present in *Training Ain't Performance* is backed by either excellent research and theory references or documented, professional practice. We place all of our references and additional resources at the end of the book in the For Further Reading section.

- *A highly interactive style.* We believe that the best way to derive applicable skills and knowledge from a book is to become actively engaged with the authors. That's why you will be continually questioned, challenged, and encouraged to participate. Please play along. You'll come out the winner as a result of your meaningful engagement.

- *A focus on application to the job.* While we have spent a great deal of our time studying human performance at work, we have invested an even greater amount of time applying what we've learned to real-world projects. A combined 70 years in the business of improving performance have taught us the wisdom of keeping our feet solidly on the ground when dealing with the world of work and its many challenges.

- *Most of all, a lifetime of learning to share with you. Training Ain't Performance* isn't about telling you what's right and wrong. It's about holding a conversation with you, even though we are not face to face. We are passionate about successful workplace learning and performance. It has taken us a long time to get to where we are today in both the understanding and practice of improving human performance. If, in our conversation together, we can help cut down your learning time, then we will have achieved one of our main goals.

With this initial start, are you ready to launch yourself further into this volume? Then, let's move on to the next chapter.

Chapter 2

What's in a Word?

Chapter Highlights:

◆ Vocabulary lesson on "familiar terms"
◆ Discussion of what's in this book and why

Let's Talk About Training, Learning, and Performance

In the companion volume to this one, *Telling Ain't Training*, we started off by defining some key terms:

- *Training*—structured activities focused on getting people to consistently reproduce behaviors without variation, but with increasingly greater efficiency (automatically) even if conditions around them change (e.g., catching a football regardless of speed, range, height, and weather conditions)
- *Instruction*—structured activities that aim at learners being able to generalize beyond the specifics of what has been taught (e.g., spotting safety violations in new workplace settings)
- *Education*—the range of structured and unstructured activities that result in the building of general mental models and values (e.g., acting as a good citizen in a democratic society; sizing up a potentially profitable business opportunity).

We linked these all to "learning," the outcome of these activities, defining it as change in our cognitive (mental) structures that leads to the potential to exhibit new, desirable behaviors. From there, we proceeded to the trainer's (also workplace instructor's or educator's) mantra: "learner-centered and performance-based." *Telling Ain't Training* went on to help readers bring this mantra to life by focusing on how learners process information and transform learning into performance outcomes. It then provided a research-based, easy-to-apply model for designing effective learning (or transforming telling to training); a plethora of effective, interactive learner-centered, performance-based learning designs; and models for testing. It then separated myth-based, counterproductive, but unfortunately common beliefs in training from research-based, effective learning principles.

All of this laid the foundation for converting the dreaded and relatively useless practice of telling (or transmission) into training (or transformation). Its purpose was to help readers develop sound training. This is good, isn't it?

Of course. But what if, as in the case of Melvyn, they have learned and still don't perform as desired? What do you do then?

Aha! Now we're saying that the training was great but nothing changed with respect to our business goals. Something was obviously missing! It's time for a new vocabulary outlook and roadmap.

A Basic Performance Vocabulary: The Terms of the Trade

There are a lot of jargony terms and words floating about in the human performance improvement universe. Being able to clearly define the key ones is extremely useful. You can communicate more clearly and decrease both ambiguity and confusion. In this chapter, we offer you a selected menu of useful terms to taste, swallow, and digest: behavior, accomplishment, performance, worth and value, along with a couple of combinations of these useful words.

BEHAVIOR

First, let's get beyond the negative connotation of "behavior" and "learning to behave." In the workplace performance setting, behavior refers to something a person does that involves an action, usually in response to some internal or external stimulation. In the list below, check off the items that you consider to be consistent with this definition:

- ☐ 1. Singing a song
- ☐ 2. Talking to another person
- ☐ 3. Mentally adding a column of figures
- ☐ 4. Winning a Grammy for a song

How did you fare? Numbers 1 and 2 are obvious examples of behavior—of "a person doing something that involves an action." It is also in response to some stimulation, either external (e.g., someone asked for a song; a person spoke to you) or internal (e.g., a feeling of joy that stimulated the singing; a need to find the closest restroom). Choice 3 is a bit trickier because it's internal. Nevertheless, adding up columns of numbers mentally is what we call a "covert" or hidden action—a doing of something—and is stimulated by the column of figures to be totaled. Number 4, however, is not "something a person does." It is the *result* of behavior (writing or singing/recording a song), not the behavior itself. There will be more about this later.

ACCOMPLISHMENT

When you employ this term, you are no longer dealing with behavior. Rather, what you have in an accomplishment is the outcome of the behavior. Choose the correct words in the following sentence: Writing a poem is (a behavior/an accomplishment); the poem is (a behavior/an accomplishment).

The act of writing is the behavior part. The poem itself is the accomplishment.

The distinction between these two terms, behavior and accomplishment, is crucial to the rest of this book. So let's stay with it for another moment to be sure we're all talking the same terms. You'll see how important the difference between the two is later when we discuss performance.

In the following list of items, check off only the accomplishments:

- ☐ **1. Run a marathon**
- ☐ **2. Completed a marathon in three hours 40 minutes**
- ☐ **3. Met sales goal**
- ☐ **4. Chose between two applicants**
- ☐ **5. Filled a position**

It's great to run a marathon and it's important to select between two applicants, but items 1 and 4 are behaviors. They are "something a person does." On the other hand, items 2—marathon completed, 3—sales goal met, and 5—position filled are results of behaviors. These are accomplishments.

To close out on the distinction between these two terms, behavior is what disappears once it has been done; accomplishment is what remains once the behavior disappears. Here is an example: "After exercising for three months, I could see my tight abs." Select the correct ending from the following selection.

1. Exercising for three months is the (behavior/accomplishment).
2. Tight abs is the (behavior/accomplishment).

Pat yourself on the back if you selected "behavior" for item 1 and "accomplishment" for item 2. The exercise disappears; the abs remain.

PERFORMANCE

Ah, the all-important term—performance. This word has been used in many ways, from acting in the theater to measured results on the sports field. We speak about the performance of a stock and of an employee. For our purposes, when we are dealing with human performance in the workplace, we operationally define the term *performance* as follows:

> Performance is a function of both the behavior and accomplishment of a person or group of people. Performance includes the actions of a person or people and the result of the action or actions.

Thus, performance includes activities and outcomes—behaviors and accomplishments. Let's check your understanding of all three terms. Place a B beside the items below that are simply behaviors, an A beside the accomplishment items, and a P next to those representing performance.

_____ 1. **They danced until dawn.**
_____ 2. **The completed audit report sat on the desk.**
_____ 3. **It took three swings at bat to finally hit the home run.**
_____ 4. **They discussed the case.**
_____ 5. **He won the Nobel prize.**
_____ 6. **After experimenting with numerous drug combinations, she found the cure.**
_____ 7. **Years of hard work led to recognition.**

Now to provide feedback on your performance:

- Items 1 and 4 are behaviors—examples of doing with no accomplishments indicated.
- Items 2 and 5 provide examples of accomplishments. There are no indications of the behavior required.
- Items 3, 6, and 7 deal with performance. They include both behaviors and the resultant accomplishments.

Concluding discussion on this term, you can now assess your own performance. Select the correct options from the following statements.

1. I analyzed each of the seven items above and selected answers for each. This was an example of (behavior/accomplishment/performance).
2. I got 100 percent of them correct. This was (a behavior/an accomplishment/a performance).

3. By carefully reading each of the seven items and checking the definitions, I was able to achieve a perfect score. This is an example of my (behavior/accomplishment/performance).

And the correct answers: 1 = behavior; 2 = accomplishment; 3 = performance. We're sure you've now got these terms all clear. You'll be seeing them frequently throughout the remainder of *Training Ain't Performance* and a great deal elsewhere beyond these pages.

WORTH AND VALUE

Suppose we offered you a flawless, two-carat, perfectly cut diamond—the genuine article, no fooling—for $50. Right here and right now. Would you buy it? Of course you would and why not? In a flash, you would compare the diamond's value to the cost and you would say, "It's worth it!"

That's what worth is all about, comparing value (what buyers would pay for it) to cost. More technically, we can state that:

$$\text{Worth} = \frac{\text{Value}}{\text{Cost}} \quad \text{or} \quad W = \frac{V}{C}$$

This is a benefit (value) to cost ratio. If the value is $20,000 and the cost only $50, the worth is:

$$W = \frac{V}{C}$$
$$= \frac{\$20,000}{\$50}$$
$$= 400{:}1$$

Wow! It's certainly worth it.

Later, you'll encounter worth and value combined with other words to form useful performance improvement concepts and tools. Three of these are:

- **Worthy performance,** which means performance (the combination of behaviors and accomplishments) that is "worth it" from a cost or expenditure perspective (not noble such as "worthy knight" or "worthy deed"). Worthy performance (P_W) is performance in which the value it generates is substantially greater than the cost of achieving it.
- **Valued accomplishment,** which means that the result obtained is one that the organization, the person performing, and all other significant stakeholders view as being desirable.
- **Worth analysis,** which is an analytical procedure that has you calculating the extent to which there is a financial benefit for closing the gap between current and desired performance levels.

This was quite an array of meanings and uses of *worth* and its cousin *value*. To help stabilize the meaning in your mind, here's a brief challenge exercise. Match the terms in the left-hand column with the definitions in the right-hand column. We have added some extra definitions to heighten the challenge. All you have to do is write the definition number in the blank beside the term.

Term	Definition
_____ Worth	1. Something a person does that involves an action, usually in response to some stimulation.
_____ Value	2. A ratio of value compared with cost.
_____ Worthy performance	3. The amount buyers consider appropriate to pay for a good, a commodity, or a service; the right price.
_____ Worth analysis	4. The result of a behavior; what remains after the behavior is completed.
	5. A function of both the behavior and accomplishment of a person or group of people.
	6. Performance in which the value it generates is substantially greater than the cost of achieving it.
	7. An analytical procedure that allows you to calculate the extent to which there is a financial benefit for closing the gap between current and desired performance levels.

Now for your results. The correct responses are: 2, 3, 6, and 7. This was a bit tough and confusing. Reward yourself well if you got them all right. If not, no concern because you'll be encountering these terms as we move from a training perspective to one much more focused on worthy performance.

The Key to Performance Improvement: A New Mantra

It's fairly common to have one of your clients—internal or external—come to you and say, "I've got a training problem. My [fill in with the name of any group] is/are not getting the right results. They . . . [story continues about the client's woes]. So I need you to give them training on . . . [list of specifics]."

With infinite variations, we encounter this type of request over and over again. Let's stop for a moment to analyze the scenario. Begin with the first sentence: "I've got a training problem." What's wrong with it? Select your answer.

☐ 1. The people aren't performing well so training is appropriate.
☐ 2. The sentence is grammatically incorrect.
☐ 3. Training is not a problem. It's a solution.

The correct answer is a very loud and clear number 3. The statement "I've got a training problem," is akin to saying I have an aspirin problem. Training, like aspirin, is a prescribed solution. There is a leap of faith in that sentence that presupposes a training intervention, even though it may not be appropriate or sufficient to achieve desired performance results. Remember: *Training ain't performance!*

This leads us to our performance improvement mantra: "cause-conscious, not solution-focused." Meditate for a moment. Visualize the scene. Your customer is right in front of you, pouring out her trials and tribulations. The more she speaks, the more convinced and committed she becomes about her needed training intervention. Yet, research on workplace performance tells us that training only works where there are skill and/or knowledge deficiencies. Many other factors affect performance. These may include anything and everything from the state of the economy to poor supervision to lack of access to equipment to "just-don't-care" attitudes, with an imposing array of other possibilities to be considered.

Still meditating, take a deep breath as your customer continues her explanation and think, "cause-conscious, not solution-focused . . . cause-conscious, not solution-focused." Now keep on listening to the customer for clues about where the true problem might be. Practice with the following scenarios. In each case, select what you think might potentially be the real cause.

1. "My people need training on selling skills. They don't seem to be able to position our new product against the competition." (They lack selling skills./The company hasn't defined the product's market position clearly.)

2. "This is a real training problem. My customer service agents keep cutting the customers off in their explanations. They don't take enough time to listen." (They lack training in listening skills./They are measured on how many calls they handle and how quickly they handle them.)

3. "This is a training issue. Even though they are technically savvy, our systems engineers don't check out every facet of the installations. We're experiencing a high volume of customer callbacks and increased customer dissatisfaction." (They lack technical skills and knowledge./They lack appropriate work standards and job aids.)

You didn't receive enough information in each case to make a clear diagnosis, but we suspect that you looked beyond the customer "training" request and at least considered the other possible cause in each case. This is what we mean by being cause-conscious, not solution-focused—not just accepting the first, most obvious, and superficial intervention, but immediately adopting an analytical frame of mind that will ultimately lead to desired customer and organizational benefits.

Meanwhile, you have to move out of the meditation mode and respond in a helpful, supportive manner to your client. And here are your words: "I can help you solve your problem." With this statement, did you . . .

	Yes	No
1. Agree to provide training?	☐	☐
2. Offer your support?	☐	☐
3. Provide a launch pad for conducting more in-depth analysis?	☐	☐
4. Act arrogantly or aggressively to put your client down?	☐	☐

With your simple sentence (which we learned from Joe Harless, one of the top performance consulting experts), you have set your client at ease; offered support in a friendly, helpful manner; set the stage to delve into the true issues affecting performance; and fulfilled the requirements of your mantra: cause-conscious, not solution-focused. Bravo!

Where Does Technology Fit in All This?

Because we are still in the early stages of *Training Ain't Performance*, let's take the opportunity to position your performance mission with respect to technology. What is technology? Modern definitions of the term suggest that it is the application of scientific and organized knowledge to solve practical problems. Technology is not just machinery and tools—the artifacts produced by technology. It is also the application of knowledge derived from scientific research and documented professional practice to achieve desirable outcomes. The field of human performance technology (HPT) is just that: applying what science and respectable professional practice have discovered that can help us achieve valued performance from and through people.

Your mission, and through *Training Ain't Performance,* ours as well, is to apply these discoveries appropriately to meet your own and your clients' desired goals.

Machines, computers, software systems, knowledge management tools, e-learning, and all other technological solutions are only as good as their appropriateness to the need. They, too, are solutions. *Training Ain't Performance* is taking you on a course that begins by asking you to hear the client's need (reactively via a request or proactively through your own observations and investigations), determine the what and why of the performance gap, and then prescribe the best, most suitable basket of interventions possible. You are donning the performance consulting mantle. Technology, as with all other solutions, fits in as appropriate. E-learning, knowledge management, or blended solutions will all find their place as you go about discovering what is necessary and—equally important from a time and cost perspective—sufficient. Technology ain't performance either.

What's in This Book and Why?

The overall goal of this book is for you to identify gaps in workplace performance that are related to what people do, identify the factors associated with each of the gaps, and then select and help implement the appropriate performance interventions. In other words, transform your own role to that of "performance consultant." That's quite a mission and a mouthful. However, it happens to be a very worthwhile cause. As part of this mission, it is essential not to spring to the default intervention of "training" every time there is a performance gap. Consider these three statements:

> "American industries annually spend more than $100 billion on training . . . not more than 10 percent of the expenditures actually result in transfer to the job." (Baldwin and Ford, 1988, page 63; reconfirmed by Ford and Weissbein, 1997)

> "Most of the investment in organizational training . . . is wasted because most of the knowledge and skills gained (well over 80 percent by some estimates) is not fully applied by these employees on the job." (Broad and Newstrom, 1992, page ix)

> "Companies that have transformed their training departments into learning and performance support organizations have had the greatest success in obtaining outstanding results from employees. When comparing companies that strongly support their people with those that are low supporters, over a 10 year period, findings show that sales growth is more than twice as high; profits, four times higher; profit margins, double; and share earnings more than double." (Stolovitch, 2000, page 3)

These affirmations offer considerable food for thought...and fuel for action. We are committed to working with you collaboratively to avoid knee-jerk-solution reactions to performance issues. We want to do this in a friendly, conversational style with lots of opportunity to reflect and perform. With these as our overall guidelines, here are the principles that we have applied in putting this book together:

- *Focus on you.* Much as we love the content, it has little meaning or value unless you can absorb it, accept it, and apply it.
- *Apply the best learning and performance principles* to ensure that you "get it" and can use what we provide. This includes training on basic tools and models; instruction on the application of principles, templates, and guidelines; and education to establish general mental models and values with respect to human performance improvement along with strong rationales for these.

- *Provide examples.* Don't just show models and tools for analyzing and solving performance problems; provide actions that bring them to life and include realistic and meaningful examples. This book includes such models and tools and also illustrates their use. The examples bring the models to life and render them concrete.

- *Personalize each major point.* To the extent possible, we get you involved in either applying principles, tools, and templates to your issues or considering how you might apply them.

- *Provide a roadmap for engineering effective performance (EEP).* We have included an EEP model that is operational. With adaptations, or as is, you can use it in your work immediately.

- *Position training with respect to performance.* Training, in the broadest sense of encompassing all deliberate interventions designed to trigger and support learning, is important for the performance of people. Rarely, however, is it sufficient, and, sometimes, it's not even necessary to attain desired behaviors and accomplishments. We have ensured that training is suitably positioned with clear reasons for why it should or should not be used and how it can best be supported to obtain maximum value from the training investment.

- *Provide a set of performance interventions for immediate use.* This will let you get started right away as a performance consultant—a role we highly encourage you to adopt.

- *Clarify what performance consulting is as well as the role of the performance consultant.* You may not know it yet, but *Training Ain't Performance* is largely about expanding your role (and your organization's mission if you are in a training group) to encompass the practice of performance consulting. You will find that we define the professional activities of the performance consultant and provide some guidelines and tools for the job.

- *Demonstrate the value of focusing on performance.* To compete and be successful in today's work environment, you have to show your worth to the organization in terms key decision makers value. We provide a whole section on calculating the return-on-investment (ROI) of your performance interventions. We also refer to ROI periodically throughout the chapters because this is a key, practical, and increasingly important aspect of performance improvement.

- *Present both truths and myths about performance* so that you can help others either make appropriate decisions about learning and performance or support your initiatives. With the best of intentions, managers and training professionals—even seasoned performance consultants—apply and preach unfounded or counterproductive principles. Armed with a strong research and/or theory foundation, you can better defend your decisions and counter those that are misleading. We have selected a number of myths and included them for you along with documented explanations. Forewarned is forearmed.

◆ *Conclude with some final reflections and supportive comments* to help you apply and maintain what we have shared and learned together. Like any book, once it comes to an end, it goes up on a shelf and soon joins the ranks of all the others you have visited. We'd like to part company with you from this book with a message of encouragement and support so that we can continue maintaining the dialogue.

As with *Telling Ain't Training*, we have not interrupted the flow of the conversation with references. You'll find a resource section with suggestions for further reading at the back of the book.

Remember This

Let's close this chapter with a review of key points. However, we must adhere to our performance principles. And a key one is that you must perform—behave and accomplish. We'll be right there with you to provide feedback.

Select the correct word or phrase in parenthesis that best fits each of the following statements.

1. In training, the mantra to retain and apply is (learner-centered, performance based/content-centered, instructor-based).
2. In performance, the mantra to retain and apply is (cause-conscious, not solution-focused/solution-conscious, not cause-focused).
3. Analyzing a court decision of great importance to our company is an example of (a behavior/an accomplishment).
4. Increased customer satisfaction ratings and decreased complaint escalations are examples of (behaviors/accomplishments).
5. Performance is a function of (cause and effect/behavior and accomplishment).
6. Worthy performance in the context of this book refers to (noble achievements/ behaviors and accomplishments of greater value than their cost).
7. The best response to a client's request for training is ("I can help you solve your problem"/"Are you sure you need training?").
8. Technology is (machines and tools derived from science and practical experience/the application of scientific and organized knowledge to solve practical problems).

9. Most of the investment in organizational training is (wasted/wisely spent).
10. The focus of this entire volume is (performance/you).

Here are our answers and comments.

1. In training, the mantra to retain and apply is learner-centered, performance-based. Too much of training is content-focused. The instructor often is like a high priest of the content, concerned with looking and sounding credible. The mission appears to be that of covering all the content in the allowable timeframe. This is transmission. We learn little from telling. The much more productive approach is learner-centered and performance-based. The mission is to transform the learner and to provide learners with the opportunity to perform—to demonstrate learning and achieve desired learning outcomes.

2. In performance, the mantra to retain and apply is cause-conscious, not solution-focused. Without an adequate diagnosis of the gap between desired and current performance, any solution you select or offer is a guess. By being cause-conscious and finding out all the factors affecting the gap, solutions naturally present themselves.

3. Analyzing a court decision of great importance to our company is an example of a behavior. The action of analyzing means that you are doing something in response to a stimulation (the court decision). We have no idea about what has been accomplished as a result of the activity.

4. Increased customer satisfaction ratings and decreased complaint escalations are examples of accomplishments. We don't know what behaviors led to these desired outcomes—perhaps the company launched an easier-to-use and better-performing product—but happy outcomes are clear.

5. Performance is a function of behavior and accomplishment. You do something and accomplish something. Both are necessary. The more efficient the behavior (least cost, least resources, least time) and the more effective the accomplishment (highest degree of desirable outcome), the better the performance.

6. Worthy performance in the context of this book refers to behaviors and accomplishments of greater value than their cost. No further comment is required.

7. The best response to a client's request for training is, "I can help you solve your problem." The message is friendly, encouraging, and supportive. It shows interest, but does not promise training—a professional response.

8. Technology is the application of scientific and organized knowledge to solve practical problems. Machines and tools are artifacts created on the basis of science and/or craft. They may be the fruits of technological invention, but they are not technology itself.

9. Most of the investment in organizational training is wasted. This doesn't mean that training has no value or place in improving workplace performance. What the research literature suggests is that training is often selected as the intervention of choice when the problem (gap) is not skills- or knowledge-related. And even when appropriate, research on human performance at work suggests that, alone, training is rarely sufficient to achieve lasting workplace results.

10. The focus of this entire volume is you. Although our content deals with issues of performance, you are why we have put fingers to keyboard. If you succeed in applying what has taken us a lifetime to learn, you will have made us successful.

This chapter has been long and has talked about a number of issues and principles. Time to put you to work. A case has just come up. The client is waiting for you to proceed to the next chapter.

Chapter 3

The Performance System

- "I need a training program" game and debriefing
- The relationship between the external environment and human performance requirements
- An organizational human performance system

"I Need a Training Program . . ."

The fact that you picked up this book and have come this far suggests that you have a strong desire to help clients achieve their desired performance goals. Therefore, by the powers vested in us (which we have given ourselves), we now dub you performance consultant at ProtoPlasmics Biotech. You're new to the job. You convinced those who hired you to change the job title from training specialist to performance consultant. You must have been persuasive because you got both the well-paying job and the new title. Now you're going to have to demonstrate results. Don't worry. We're standing by as your consultants. Our fee is included in the price of the book.

Here is the setup. A client, the manager of vial inspection, sealing, and packaging, has a problem. She has come to get your help. In a moment, you'll enter into the case. Before you do, here are some instructions.

- Read each section of the case. These are labeled section 1, 2, 3, 4, and 5.

- In sections 1, 2, and 4, you will be faced with choices. On page 26 you will find a worksheet. Select your choice(s) from the options given each time, and enter it/them on the worksheet in the appropriate spaces in the column entitled "My choice." We will guide you as you proceed.
- On the worksheet, you will see a column entitled "Score." Along the way, in sections 3 and 5, you will receive feedback on your selected choices and be attributed points for them. Enter the scores on the worksheet when you receive them.
- Sorry, but there's no going back to change a selection or peeking ahead. We're trying to make this realistic. Play along to discover some useful performance principles.

SECTION 1. I'VE GOT A TRAINING PROBLEM!

So here you are, the new performance consultant at ProtoPlasmics Biotech, which produces genetically based, disease-fighting products. The market is fiercely competitive and the industry highly regulated. Laws and regulations control production, supply, and distribution of these powerful, avant-garde drugs. Alexandra Hill, manager of vial inspection, sealing, and packaging, has come to you to develop a training program for her department. Her group is responsible for final inspection and proper sealing and packaging of all vials of their high-demand tumor-fighting drug. The product is sensitive, and each vial must be inspected, sealed, and packaged according to tight requirements before it can be sent on to distribution. The employees, most with—at a minimum—an associate degree in chemistry or biology, inspect, place the final seal on, and package the vials.

There are three work shifts per 24 hours, each with the same number of workers. Each shift has three supervisors: one for inspection, one for sealing, and a third who oversees packaging. Workers rotate through the three jobs for maximum flexibility. Alexandra is in charge of the complete vial inspection, sealing, and packaging operation for all shifts.

The 8 a.m. to 4 p.m. shift produces, on average, 1,000 ready-to-distribute packages. The 4 p.m. to midnight shift is close with 980. However, the graveyard shift, midnight to 8 a.m., produces an average of only 720 ready-to-go packages. Alexandra has discovered that the quality assurance department regularly finds problems with this shift in vial quality, proper sealing, and packaging standards' violations—sometimes as high as 6 percent. This has created large cost and regulatory problems. She wants a training program for the graveyard shift workers.

Given what you have learned, which of the following best reflects your viewpoint? Choose only one.

a. This group needs training in inspection, sealing, and packaging. You will have to meet with Alexandra's team to determine necessary content and to design a learner-centered, performance-based training program.

b. This seems to be a motivation issue, not one of training. You have to explore the dampening effects of late-night work.

c. This is a performance issue, but maybe not one that calls for training. You need to know more.

◆ Go to the worksheet on page 26. Enter the letter of your selected choice in the "My choice" column beside "The problem."

◆ Once you have entered your selection, continue to read.

SECTION 2. QUESTIONS: TELL ME MORE

You feel you require more information. You meet with Alexandra, but discover that she is so busy, she only has time to answer four of your questions. From the list below, select your four questions.

a. How soon do you need the training program up and running?

b. How many workers do you want trained?

c. Do the workers on the graveyard shift know how to do the job?

d. Do graveyard shift workers have other tasks besides inspecting, sealing, and packaging vials?

e. What budget have you allocated for the training?

f. Do workers receive specific information during or after the shift on how well they are performing compared with a standard or with other shifts?

g. Do you think your graveyard shift workers like their work or their shift time?

h. What happens to the workers when they are identified as having made an error?

i. Does late-night work decrease worker motivation?

j. Were graveyard shift workers able to perform as well as other shift workers when they were initially assigned to their shift?

◆ Go to the worksheet on page 26. Enter the letters of your selected choices, one under the other, in the four spaces of the "My choice" column beside "The questions." Remember, you are limited to four questions.

◆ Once you have entered your selections, continue to the next section, which gives you feedback and points for your choices.

SECTION 3. FEEDBACK ON YOUR SELECTIONS

So far, you have entered five selections on your worksheet. Time for us to review what you have been doing and offer feedback. Read each of the choices below. Don't skip any. On your worksheet (page 26), enter the points attributed to each of your own selections. You may not agree with our feedback. However, as your consultants, this is how we view the situation. Play along, please, in the spirit of true collaboration.

The Problem

a. *This group needs training in inspection, sealing, and packaging. You will have to meet with Alexandra's team to determine necessary content and design a learner-centered, performance-based training program.* Whoa! True, Alexandra said she wants training. But you don't have enough information to decide that they lack skills and/or knowledge. Too quick a decision. **Give yourself 0 points.**

b. *This seems to be a motivation issue, not one of training. You have to explore the dampening effects of late-night work.* The other two shifts appear to be doing much better. Seems like a reasonable assumption. **Give yourself 2 points.**

c. *This is a performance issue, but maybe not one that calls for training. You need to know more.* So far, given what you have learned to date, this is your wisest choice. You really need much more information. **Give yourself 10 points.**

The Questions

a. *How soon do you need the training program up and running?* This question suggests that training is the appropriate intervention. You haven't established this yet. **Give yourself 0 points.**

b. *How many workers do you want trained?* Same remark as the one immediately above. You imply that training is required. Too hasty a decision! **Give yourself 0 points.**

c. *Do the workers on the graveyard shift know how to do the job?* In other words, do they possess sufficient skills and knowledge to meet performance standards? This would be great to know, but not by asking the boss. You would have to verify by observing or testing the workers themselves. Bosses, like parents, have biased opinions and while their answers are interesting, you can't wholly rely on them. **Give yourself 2 points.**

d. *Do graveyard shift workers have other tasks besides inspecting, sealing, and packaging vials?* Excellent question. This is a factual question, which the manager can answer. It will let you know if there are tasks workers must perform that interfere with the three primary responsibilities. **Give yourself 10 points.**

e. *What budget have you allocated for the training?* Dangerous question. You have not established whether or not training is even necessary. The only good information you can derive here is how important she views the problem by how much she is willing to spend. **Give yourself 2 points.**

f. *Do workers receive specific information during or after the shift on how well they are performing compared with a standard or with other shifts?* This is an important question! What if the standards of performance have not been communicated? Perhaps they receive no feedback on their productivity and performance quality. This is a fact-based question to which the manager can reply. **Give yourself 10 points.**

g. *Do you think your graveyard shift workers like their work or their shift time?* This is an opinion question. Unless a specific survey of workers was undertaken, the manager would only be guessing, although she may have heard some complaints or comments. Best find this out from the workers themselves. **Give yourself 1 point.**

h. *What happens to workers when you find they have made an error?* This is a good fact-based question that focuses on the consequences of poor performance. This will help to pinpoint the problem cause or causes. **Give yourself 10 points.**

i. *Does late-night work decrease worker motivation?* This only elicits the manager's opinion or bias. You would have to go to the workers themselves and probe to discover the answer. **Give yourself 0 points**.

j. *Were graveyard shift workers able to perform as well as other shift workers when they were initially assigned to their shift?* This factual question, based on entry-level performance data, is an excellent one. If they were able to perform, then this is not a skills and knowledge issue. Hence, training would be inappropriate. **Give yourself 10 points.**

- Make sure you have entered your points in the "Score" column beside each selection. You should have five selections and points.
- Continue to make your last choice in Section 4, which follows.

SECTION 4. THE INTERVENTION

You decided to ask the following four questions. Here's what you received as responses:

Q.d: *Do graveyard shift workers have other tasks besides inspecting, sealing, and packaging vials?*

A: The short answer is "no." The three tasks they have to do are important ones that demand full attention. Like the other shifts, they rotate from one task to the next over the course of a month. They are not given any other tasks.

Q.f: *Do workers receive specific information during or after the shift on how well they are performing compared with a standard or with other shifts?*

A: When workers first arrive, we train them in a special section dedicated to training. The demands are naturally reduced, and our speed standards are lower. We show them what to look for when inspecting and point out common defects. We have them sealing according to company standards, and they get to see all kinds of improper seals. They also do packaging and practice with various types of packages because these can vary depending on where we're shipping. They are taught and guided by experienced trainers. When they leave, we tell them what we expect from their work. They then go to the regular inspection, sealing, and packaging area and are assigned tasks and watched closely by the supervisors. They are informed when they are making errors.

Q.h: *What happens to workers when you find they have made an error?*

A: If they make a mistake—pass a vial with a defect, improperly seal a vial, or screw up the packaging—the supervisor who catches the mistake takes the vial or package and shows it to the work team so they all get to see it. This lets them know they are being watched and provides an example of what not to do. When the shift doesn't produce enough final packages, a supervisor announces this at shift end and lets them know that they must work more quickly next time. If their productivity is good, they sometimes get donuts with their coffee or two minutes longer on their breaks as rewards.

Q.j: *Were graveyard shift workers able to perform as well as other shift workers when they were initially assigned to their shift?*

A: As far as I know, "yes." Everyone has to be up to speed and capable before we assign someone to a shift. We assign based on worker preferences as much as possible. A lot of our workers on the midnight shift want and request these hours.

Given the answers to your four questions, you now have to decide what intervention you will recommend. Select what you consider to be the best choice from the options below.

a. *This is a training problem.* You will design a training program that covers key skills and knowledge and refreshes workers on common errors as well as ways to increase productivity. You'll build in lots of practice.

b. *This is a discipline problem.* You will work with supervisors to tighten up their observation and be tougher when production falls below that of the other shifts.

c. *This is an expectations and feedback problem.* Nowhere did you hear what the specific standards of performance are. You will review standards documents, work with Alexandra and all supervisors to establish appropriate standards, and develop a feedback system so that each worker receives continuous information on how she or he is performing compared with time and accuracy standards. You will create a brief training program for supervisors on giving feedback and rewarding exemplary performance.

   d. *This is a motivation problem.* The tasks are repetitive and demand constant attention to small details. Over time, you believe that it becomes monotonous and leads to distraction, especially late at night. You will develop a program for supervisors on how to motivate their workers to achieve high performance on repetitive tasks. You will also work with them in the areas of interpersonal relations and sensitivity.

◆ Turn to the worksheet on page 26. Enter the letter of your selected choice in the space under "My choice," next to "The intervention."

◆ When you have entered your selection, continue reading Section 5 below.

SECTION 5. FEEDBACK ON YOUR INTERVENTION CHOICE

   a. *This is a training problem.* You seem to be stuck, by default, in the training-solution paradigm. The employees have already been through training and had to demonstrate that they could do the job. No lack of skills and knowledge equals no training. **Give yourself 0 points**. (Remember, there is no such thing as a "training problem.")

   b. *This is a discipline problem.* This is an assumption with little to back it up. By increasing discipline, you also increase stress. You may obtain a brief spike in productivity, but the long-term effects may be greater anxiety with a negative impact on performance, absenteeism, and turnover. **Give yourself 0 points.**

   c. *This is an expectations and feedback problem.* Given what you have learned to date, this is an excellent choice. They may have been aware of expectations when they started the shift work, but this no longer seems to be the case. At no time have you been told what exactly is required in terms of productivity, only comparisons with other shifts. Also, feedback on performance appears to be focused on individual errors. An end-of-shift announcement, when workers are preparing to leave, is the only information given on performance. Donuts and a two-minute-longer break are presumed to be a reward—but no specifics. Clarifying and establishing unambiguous standards will be helpful. Specific, individual feedback will allow workers to monitor themselves. Improving supervisory feedback skills will also foster better performance. **Give yourself 20 points.**

   d. *This is a motivation problem.* While it is true that repetitive tasks can become monotonous and lead to errors and slowdowns, this would apply equally to all shifts. Many of the late-night workers requested this shift. It may not hurt to help supervisors improve their interpersonal skills and sensitivity, but this is a round-about way of dealing with an immediate productivity and error issue. **Give yourself 5 points.**

◆ Make sure you have entered your points in the "Score" column beside your intervention selection.

◆ Total your score and enter it in the "Total" space. The maximum possible total score is 70.

WORKSHEET

This worksheet is for you to enter your selections and points for the ProtoPlasmics Biotech case. Enter appropriate letters and point values as instructed.

ProtoPlasmics Biotech case		My choice	Score
The problem			
The questions	Q1		
	Q2		
	Q3		
	Q4		
The intervention			
Total			

DEBRIEFING THE PROTOPLASMICS BIOTECH CASE

You have just completed what could very well have been a true case. The client came to you, the performance consultant, with a problem and a solution—training. Has this happened to you before? If you are in a training function, your answer will most likely be yes. Also notice how the choice of questions to ask your customer is extremely important. Did you identify anything that united all the high-point questions—one characteristic they shared? Please return to page 21 for a moment and review questions d, f, h, and j. Check off the common characteristics they share:

☐ **They are all short.**
☐ **They are all long.**
☐ **They all require an opinion answer.**
☐ **They all require a factual answer.**

They all require a factual answer. This is what the manager can tell you with any high degree of reliability. Compare these with questions c, g, and i, which all ask for an opinion. If you truly wanted answers to these, what would be the best source? Check off your choice.

- ☐ **The workers**
- ☐ **The manager**
- ☐ **The supervisors**

Go to the source. If you must know how workers perform, observe them. How do they feel? Ask them. The data you obtain in this way will be far more valid than the response of a manager who is removed from the actual scene.

With respect to the other questions, a, b, and e, these were also factual, but focused purely on the training solution: number of trainees, budget, timing. These immediately cut off all other options. Remember: Training ain't performance.

Finally, let's review the intervention options because these lead naturally to the next part of this chapter. You were offered training, discipline, expectations and feedback, and motivation. You have already reviewed the explanations for rejecting all alternatives except the one related to expectations and feedback. We hope you noticed that this choice fell out logically from the information you gathered. This is a key point in selecting appropriate performance interventions. If you take the time to analyze the performance gap systematically, asking the right questions from the right sources, the suitable intervention or basket of interventions will surface naturally. Knowing this, when you say to your customer, "I can help solve your problem," these will not be empty words.

The Performance World

The ProtoPlasmics Biotech case provides us with an opportunity to advance from this single example to a broader examination of the world of the organizational workplace and our specific role in it. What is this world? How should we view it?

Our goal, as performance consultants (whether in name or in fact), is to help our organizations or organizational clients achieve maximum desired results from people in ways all stakeholders value. Our mission is to generate worthy performance. This is both an exciting opportunity and a formidable challenge because of the complexity of organizations and the high stakes created by the global, competitive marketplace. Not every performance gap is as simple and straightforward as our ProtoPlasmics Biotech case. So let's probe more deeply.

Begin with the world outside of the organization. This external environment presents an organization with opportunities, pressures, events, and resources, as shown in Figure 3-1.

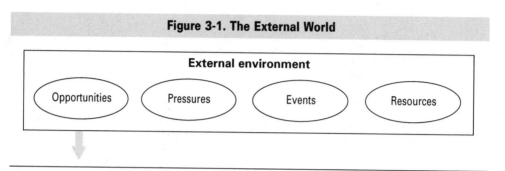

Figure 3-1. The External World

These factors in the environment stimulate the organization to generate goals and objectives—its responses to the environment. Using ProtoPlasmics Biotech as an example, these responses might be the identification of biotech market needs that offer potential for doing great good and making large profits. The company managers, in response to the environment, may come up with ideas for leveraging events in biotechnology research. The external environment offers human resources and partners to share risk and knowledge as well as suppliers of needed materials and services. The company's management must take into account competition; regulatory agencies and requirements; and the cost of capital for research, infrastructure, manufacture, distribution, and all other facets of the business.

Based on what the external world has generated in terms of goals and objectives, senior management must draw up a list of its internal requirements—what it must do to exploit the opportunities and deal with the pressures from the external environment. These internal requirements may include financial plans, technology, organizational structures, manufacturing facilities, and much more. Among these is one set of internal requirements that concerns us: human performance—what we must derive from our people. Once these standards are articulated, they trigger a number of people behaviors that result in accomplishments.

Figure 3-2 shows how all of these relate. It also indicates that behaviors and accomplishments are strongly influenced by both the external environment (what is happening out there: the economy, the job market, the competition, laws, and how the organization has decided to respond to these outside factors) and the internal environment. The internal environment consists of many influencing factors such as information, resources, incentives, the organizational culture and climate, and immediate conflicting job demands.

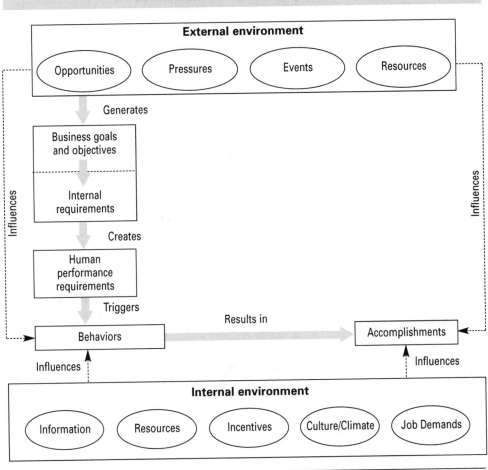

Figure 3-2. Relationship Between the External Environments and Human Performance Requirements

Accomplishments may or may not suffice. You must, therefore, monitor and verify them to determine if they are meeting business requirements (relevant even for nonbusiness systems) or are unacceptable. In the latter case, they will have to be modified.

Figure 3-3 shows the entire human performance system in action.

This is your performance world. To ensure that your client obtains the "required human performance," you have to become completely familiar with the bigger organizational picture. Keeping in mind the business goals and objectives, you must analyze the system, diagnose the performance gap, and either design or recommend the design of suitable interventions (appropriate, least cost, quickest turnaround, greatest payback).

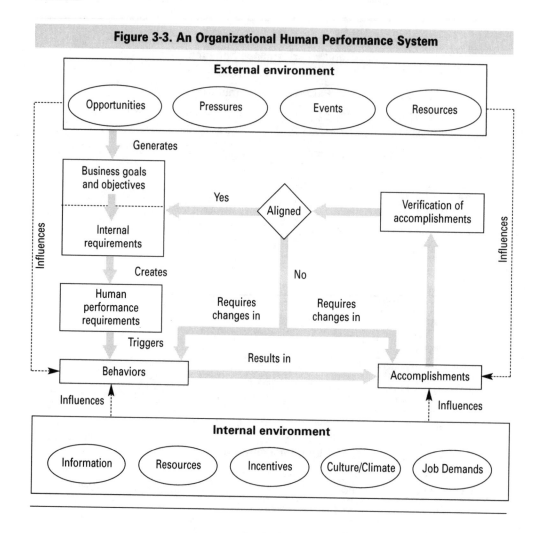

Figure 3-3. An Organizational Human Performance System

To do this requires that you adopt a *systemic* view of the organization. This means that you do not regard each element piecemeal or in isolation. You examine all the elements as they interrelate. Your viewpoint encompasses all the parts of the system working together to produce a unified, customer-desired result. How you do this operationally will emerge in a later chapter.

Time to apply what you have just learned to a small, but realistic case. If you can see your way through this case, you're well on the road to performance consulting success. Please read it carefully and underline key points.

Following our human performance system model from Figure 3-3, conduct an analysis of the situation.

Case: Harry's Diner

Harry is your brother-in-law. He owns a diner in an industrial park. His major trade is breakfast and lunch, with some traffic flow-through during the morning and afternoon (coffee, toast, sweet rolls).

Harry has been lucky in that there hasn't been much competition. But rumor has it that some fast-food franchises are eyeing the area. Harry's worried. If he doesn't keep his customers satisfied, he could lose them to a popular, nationally known fast-food establishment. So Harry's been analyzing his operations, listening to customers, and watching for problems.

One glaring problem is the toast. The short-order cooks prepare the main parts of the meals. The servers make the toast. Harry buys his bread from an Italian bakery. He has an "exclusive" with the bakery in his area. The bread arrives in full loaves (raisin, raisin-walnut, seven-grain, ciabatta). Servers slice the bread, place the slices on the conveyer toaster (heated by gas flames for a toastier flavor), and pick the toast up when it drops into the receiving pan.

When the toast is done right, customers love it. However, customers often send toast back (10 to 15 percent of the time) because the slices are too thick, too thin, too dark, too light, too cold, uneven, etc. Complaints and rejections increase during peak periods. Rejected toast holds up orders; slows down service; makes customers late; creates tensions; increases costs, waste, and rework; and is a major sore spot because Harry's toast is a big draw for the diner.

Harry's Diner experiences a 40 percent annual turnover in serving staff. So training is an important issue. Training is done on the job. A new server is teamed with an experienced one. The new server shadows, assists, and—after two to three days—is given a section.

Servers have other tasks besides making toast. They serve, make coffee, fill salt and pepper shakers, clean ketchup bottles, check bathrooms, prepare bills, and assist busboys in table cleanups and setups. They are also supposed to chat with the customers to build relationships and encourage repeat business.

Harry feels that the toast issue is a serious one and that servers need better training in making toast than they are currently getting. He has asked you to develop this training for him.

1. From the external environment, check off those elements relevant to Harry's case.

Opportunities:	Pressures:
☐ Gourmet dining	☐ Current competition
☐ Fast-food menu	☐ Potential competition
☐ Diner with character	☐ Customer fickleness

Events:	Resources:
☐ Changing demographics	☐ Lots of experienced servers
☐ Fast-food franchises scouting the area	☐ Flexible short-order cooks
☐ Tight toast market	☐ Exclusive tie-in with an Italian bakery
	☐ Servers with potential

Here's what you probably checked off:

- Diner with character (special, made-to-measure toast)
- Potential competition (popular fast-food franchises)
- Fast-food franchises scouting the area
- Exclusive tie-in with an Italian bakery
- Servers with potential.

2. Check off the most appropriate business goals and objectives for Harry's Diner.

- ☐ **Beat the current competition**
- ☐ **Gain and retain customers through excellent food service and high customer satisfaction**
- ☐ **Train servers to make toast correctly**

You most likely checked off "gain and retain . . . ." This is what Harry wants to achieve with respect to the outside environment. There currently is no competition. Training is rarely a business goal or objective.

3. Based on Harry's Diner's goals and objectives, he has a number of requirements. You are focused on the human performance subset, which in this case is:

- ☐ **Serve toast as ordered and expected to achieve high customer satisfaction**
- ☐ **Get servers to complete all work tasks before they leave**
- ☐ **Reduce annual turnover**
- ☐ **Train servers to make great toast**

You may have been tempted to go in several directions. However, in this case, there is one overriding human performance requirement: serve toast as ordered and expected with resulting customer satisfaction.

4. What behaviors and accomplishments does this requirement trigger? Check off all that apply.

Behaviors	Accomplishments
☐ Take order with no errors.	☐ Toast to customer specification.
☐ Select correct bread.	☐ Toast hot and on time.
☐ Toast bread according to specifications.	☐ Salt shakers full.
☐ Serve toast quickly.	☐ Tables ready for next customer.
☐ Serve toast hot.	☐ Bathrooms clean.
☐ Fill salt shakers.	☐ Tables cleaned and cleared quickly.

While Harry may want it all, with respect to this specific requirement, you should have checked off all of the items in the list of behaviors except for the last one, which is not related to the toast requirement. Similarly, only the first two accomplishments require checkmarks. The others have nothing to do with the toast performance issue.

5. Now to verify accomplishments. Check off the quotes that show the extent to which these are working or not.

    ☐ **"When the toast is done right, customers love it."**
    ☐ **"... customers often send toast back (10 to 15 percent of the time) ...."**
    ☐ **"... slices are too thick, too thin, too dark, too light, too cold, uneven ...."**
    ☐ **"... complaints and rejections increase during peak periods."**
    ☐ **"Rejected toast holds up orders; slows down service; makes customers late ...."**

You should have checked off every one. Harry feels that the toast issue is serious. And he's right.

6. Based on the state of the accomplishments, select (using a checkmark) the direction that you believe the data point to in Figure 3-4. In other words, are the current toast accomplishments completely aligned with business goals and objectives and internal requirements or not?

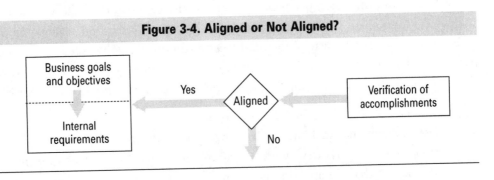

Figure 3-4. Aligned or Not Aligned?

We're sure you selected the "no" direction. Accomplishments are not aligned with the goal of "Gain and retain customers through excellent food service and high customer satisfaction." A key internal requirement is the serving of hot toast on time and according to customer specifications. Something will have to be done to change behaviors and accomplishments.

7. By analyzing the system and taking into account external influences (e.g., potential competition, types of servers, customer desires and options, Harry's bread source) and internal ones (e.g., the information servers receive,

the resources for them to do the job, incentives such as pay and tips, the diner culture and climate, the variety of job demands), you will have to determine how to help your brother-in-law, Harry. At this point, what will be your course of action to achieve desired performance results for all stakeholders (Harry, the customers, the servers)? Check off your selection.

- ☐ **Create a really good toast-making and -serving training program.**
- ☐ **Create greater motivation in the servers to achieve better results.**
- ☐ **Have the Italian bakery supply presliced breads.**
- ☐ **Tell Harry, "I can help you solve your problem," and dig more deeply to identify root causes for the performance gap.**

If you checked off "Create a really good toast-making and -serving training program," stop here and begin rereading this book right from the start. By now you should know that training ain't performance and that in this instance the performance discrepancy is probably not due to lack of toast-making and -serving skills and knowledge. They get it right most of the time.

Selecting "Create greater motivation in the servers to achieve better results" is also too hasty a decision. Who says they are not sufficiently motivated? And what about the avoidance of rework and customer complaints as a motivating factor for getting the order right. Then there are the tips for fast, accurate service. Not a good choice.

"Have the Italian bakery supply presliced bread" may sound reasonable, but if you knew more about the diner, you would reject this choice. First, the bakery does not use preservatives. The bread slices would dry out quickly. Second, each type of bread requires a different way of slicing. Dense raisin bread can be sliced thinly, but not others that are airier. Finally, one of the special features of Harry's toast is that the customer dictates the thickness. There's no way to predict how customers will order.

This leaves us with the final choice. It sums up everything we have said to date. Reassure the customer (Harry) with a promise of a solution and analyze more deeply the factors that are affecting performance. Find these and the solution will present itself. If you selected this choice, you are definitely progressing well. The next chapter will add more to your performance problem-solving capabilities.

Remember This

Chapter 2 concluded by saying, "Time to put you to work." That's what you did throughout this chapter. You did a lot of work. Now, here's a final quiz to help you retain important points. Select the correct choice in each statement below.

1. If a client comes to you with a performance improvement problem and requests training, (suspect motivation as the root cause/offer support, promise no specific solution, and dig deeper).

2. When questioning managers about worker performance, ask questions that elicit mostly (facts/opinions).

3. If you require information on worker perception, concerns, or attitudes, your best source is (the managers/the local supervisors/the workers).

4. A strong indicator that training will not produce desired performance is that workers (lack requisite skills and knowledge/could perform correctly in the past).

5. The opportunities, pressures, events, and resources of the external environment generate (business goals and objectives/a need for training).

6. Adopting a systemic view of the organization means regarding (each element as separate and independent/all elements as interrelated).

7. In an organization such as Harry's Diner it is (possible/not possible) to improve performance in a way that satisfies all stakeholders.

Ready for feedback on your choices?

1. If a client comes to you with a performance improvement problem and requests training, offer support, promise no specific solution, and dig deeper. This is a major responsibility of a performance consulting professional. Suspicions are precisely that—biased guesses. Set aside all preconceived notions, work with the client, and discover what the root factors are that must be dealt with to attain the client's goals.

2. When questioning managers about worker performance, ask questions that elicit mostly facts. While manager opinions are interesting to note, they may not accurately reflect what is happening. Their opinions may bias your own observations and findings.

3. If you require information on worker perceptions, concerns, or attitudes, your best source is the workers. If we wish to discover your personal perceptions, concerns, and attitudes, should we rely on your parents, guardians, or spouses as the major information source or should we observe and question you? Always go directly to the primary data source for the most credible information.

4. A strong indicator that training will not produce desired performance is that workers could perform correctly in the past. If workers could do it before, then it is unlikely that the issue is one of skills and knowledge. Red flag words are "refresher training," "retraining," or "motivational training." If training didn't do it the first time, be wary.

5. The opportunities, pressures, events, and resources of the external environment generate business goals and objectives. Senior management scans the outside world to identify opportunities while weighing risks. It is the conditions of the marketplace that generate the goals and market direction of the business. Training should only be triggered by a lack of required skills and knowledge to meet the goals.

6. Adopting a systemic view of the organization means regarding all elements as interrelated. Viewed systemically—as a system—all elements are perceived as interacting with all other system elements. If one element fails, it affects many others and may shut down the whole system. A human performance system consists of many elements (see Figure 3-3). If one of these is out of kilter (if, for example, behaviors are insufficient or inappropriate), the entire system suffers. That's why a systemic vision is crucial to performance improvement.

7. In an organization such as Harry's Diner, it is possible to improve performance in a way that satisfies all stakeholders. Sure, if the toast is served perfectly, customers, servers, and Harry all smile. That is our mission: engineering the performance system in ways all stakeholders value.

You have put a great deal of effort into completing this chapter. Kudos. Reward yourself. Not for too long, however. There's more work ahead in the next chapter where we examine the factors that affect performance. Here's the good news. We start by focusing on you!

Chapter 4

What's My Greatest Performance Block?

Chapter Highlights:

◆ Gilbert's Behavior Engineering Model
◆ How your performance block compares with others
◆ What managers perceive their workers' performance blocks to be
◆ Three forces: work, workplace, and worker

I Would Perform Better If . . .

Think about your current job. If you're not employed at the moment, focus on your last job and put yourself back into the environment. Imagine you are still working there. Answer the following question honestly, "Could you perform better than you are currently performing?" Even a little better?

☐ **Yes**
☐ **No**

We have posed this question to thousands of people in the workplace, from novice, entry-level junior personnel to very senior managers. We have never received a "no" answer. Everyone sees the potential for better performance.

So what's holding you back? We will offer you the first part of a sentence and then ask you to complete it with the ending that best fits you. Before we do this, a word of explanation. What's holding you back at this moment may be something very personal such as an injury or illness, an emotional issue with which you are dealing, or a specific life situation. We are asking you to put these personal concerns aside, difficult as that may be. Instead, we ask you to focus on more general, systemic issues found in the workplace. Here, then, is the statement and range of choices. *You may select (✓) only one.*

I would perform better if...

☐ 1. **I knew the exact expectations of the job and had more specific job feedback and better access to information.**
☐ 2. **I had better tools and resources to work with.**
☐ 3. **I had better financial and nonfinancial incentives/consequences for doing my work.**
☐ 4. **I received more and better training to do my job.**
☐ 5. **My personal characteristics and capacities better matched the job.**
☐ 6. **I cared more and really wanted to do my job better.**

As tempting as it might be to select more than one choice, go with the one that would provide the greatest performance boost.

Now for some feedback.

Gilbert's Behavior Engineering Model

Thomas F. Gilbert (1996) is usually considered to be the father of human performance technology. In his studies of workplace performance, he identified six major sets of factors that affect workplace performance and built them into a model. We have adapted his model slightly for the purpose of this activity, but have retained its overall meaning. The choice you checked off above represents one of the six factors identified by Gilbert, and presented graphically in Table 4-1.

Table 4-1. Gilbert's Behavior Engineering Model (adapted)

	Information	Resources	Incentives/ Consequences
Environment			
	Knowledge and Skills	Capacity	Motivation
Individual			

The three sets of factors in the top row are environmental factors. These are outside the individual performer's control. As you can see, these are:

- *Information*—especially, clear expectations of the job, clear standards, specific and timely feedback on performance with respect to expectations, and access to required information on a timely basis
- *Resources*—including tools; systems; proper procedures; easy-to-use reference manuals; adequate time; experts or expert systems; and adequate, safe facilities
- *Incentives/Consequences*—both financial and nonfinancial, including tangible and intangible rewards, recognition, promotions, and punishments, not only for oneself but also for others in the work environment.

The factors in the second row of the model refer to the individual. These are:

- *Knowledge and skills*—especially acquired through more and better training, development opportunities, work assignments, participation in seminars and conferences, and workplace education
- *Capacity*—including personal characteristics; personality traits; preferences; physical, mental, and emotional limitations; and personal constraints due to life situation or lifestyle
- *Motivation*—which encompasses the amount of value attributed to the job or an aspect of it; level of confidence to perform well; and mood, especially the one created by the work climate, culture, and atmosphere (e.g., threatening, stressful, supportive, positive).

The Gilbert Model, therefore, offers a portrait of major factors that can block (or facilitate) workplace performance. Go back to the Gilbert Model in Figure 4-1 and place a checkmark in the box that represents your greatest performance block. This checkmark should match the selection you made earlier in the list of choices about what is holding you back.

Where did you place yourself? Remember you can pick only one of the six factors to characterize your greatest performance block. Then, read ahead to see how your personal performance block compares with thousands of others who have performed the same exercise.

Dr. Peter Dean conducted this exercise with hundreds of workers, across a broad range of jobs and organizational levels internationally. So have we. His results and ours coincide remarkably. The combination of findings is displayed in Table 4-2.

Table 4-2. Gilbert's Behavior Engineering Model (adapted) with Data

	Information	Resources	Incentives/Consequences
Environment 75%	35%	26%	14%
	Knowledge and Skills	**Capacity**	**Motivation**
Individual 25%	11%	8%	6%

Where did you come out on this matrix? What is remarkable is the consistency of results both Peter Dean and we have experienced in our many applications of this brief exercise. Between 70 and 80 percent of people at work identify environmental factors as the greatest cause of why they do not perform better. Was yours an environmental factor choice as well?

Debriefing the Gilbert Model Exercise

An initial question is "Do people simply blame the outside environment rather than themselves for lack of exemplary performance?" This is a reasonable question to which there are two responses.

Response 1: When we ask managers to participate in this same exercise, but change the statement to "My workers would perform better if . . ." with the same six choices, here is what we obtain. Managers select the environmental factors 58 percent of the time and individual factors 42 percent. Notice the differences in Table 4-3.

Table 4-3. Self versus Manager Selection of Performance Blocks

	Self-selection	Manager selection
Environment	75%	58%
Individual	25%	42%

This is a significant shift to individual factors, but *environmental factors still come out higher.*

Response 2: In numerous research and professional reports, articles, and books dealing with factors affecting workplace performance, the general findings are heavily weighted to environmental factors. The greatest emphasis falls on the Information block, with lack of clarity of expectations and specific, timely feedback the most frequently cited reasons. In the For Further Reading section at the back of this book, we offer you a host of additional references on this important subject.

This leads to some important conclusions that should guide you in your performance consulting thinking.

Three Key Conclusions for Performance Consulting

Please read each of these conclusions slowly and carefully. Let their meanings sink in. Allow them to guide the way in which you view workplace performance. Gilbert stated these principles, but other experienced human performance improvement specialists have often repeated them.

- Lack of performance in the workplace is far more frequently caused by environmental rather than individual factors.

  Has this been your observation and experience?   ☐ **Yes**   ☐ **No**

- Nevertheless, we continue trying to fix the individual rather than the environment.

  Has this been your observation and experience?   ☐ **Yes**   ☐ **No**

- It is cheaper and easier to fix the environment.

  Would this be true in your circumstances?   ☐ **Yes**   ☐ **No**

If we return to Harry's Diner, do you think we may find that these principles apply? We have reproduced the Harry's Diner Case for you below.

Case: Harry's Diner

Harry is your brother-in-law. He owns a diner in an industrial park. His major trade is breakfast and lunch, with some traffic flow-through during the morning and afternoon (coffee, toast, sweet rolls).

Harry has been lucky in that there hasn't been much competition. But rumor has it that some fast-food franchises are eyeing the area. Harry's worried. If he doesn't keep his customers satisfied, he could lose them to a popular, nationally known fast-food establishment. So Harry's been analyzing his operations, listening to customers, and watching for problems.

(continued on page 42)

> **Case: Harry's Diner (continued)**
>
> One glaring problem is the toast. The short-order cooks prepare the main parts of the meals. The servers make the toast. Harry buys his bread from an Italian bakery. He has an "exclusive" with the bakery in his area. The bread arrives in full loaves (raisin, raisin-walnut, seven-grain, ciabatta). Servers slice the bread, place the slices on the conveyor toaster (heated by gas flames for a toastier flavor), and pick the toast up when it drops into the receiving pan.
>
> When the toast is done right, customers love it. However, customers often send toast back (10-15 percent of the time) because the slices are too thick, too thin, too dark, too light, too cold, uneven, etc. Complaints and rejections increase during peak periods. Rejected toast holds up orders; slows down service; makes customers late; creates tensions; increases costs, waste, and rework; and is a major sore spot because Harry's toast is a big draw for the diner.
>
> Harry's Diner experiences a 40 percent annual turnover in serving staff. So training is an important issue. Training is done on the job. A new server is teamed with an experienced one. The new server shadows, assists, and—after two to three days—is given a section.
>
> Servers have other tasks besides making toast. They serve, make coffee, fill salt and pepper shakers, clean ketchup bottles, check bathrooms, prepare bills, and assist busboys in table cleanups and setups. They are also supposed to chat with the customers to build relationships and encourage repeat business.
>
> Harry feels that the toast issue is a serious one and that servers need better training in making toast than they are currently getting. He has asked you to develop this training for him.

In light of the Gilbert Model, check off yes or no to the following questions.

		Yes	No
1.	Expectations and feedback with respect to toast service are clear, but there are other interfering expectations that may hamper servers from performing well.	☐	☐
2.	Resources may be lacking (e.g., toasters, well-designed workspace) for servers to perform well.	☐	☐
3.	Incentives and consequences are lacking for servers to perform well.	☐	☐
4.	Servers lack sufficient skills and knowledge to take toast orders, make toast, and serve toast correctly.	☐	☐
5.	Servers lack the capacity to make the toast correctly (e.g., physical/emotional/intellectual limitations).	☐	☐
6.	Servers are not motivated to make and serve the toast correctly (e.g., do not value perfect toast, lack toast-making confidence, experience a negative mood about making and serving toast correctly).	☐	☐

Now for the feedback and discussion on this exercise.

	Yes	No
1. Expectations and feedback with respect to toast service are clear, but there are other interfering expectations that may hamper servers from performing well.	☑	☐

Every server understands what the customer expects: toast according to the way it was ordered. Feedback is also clear, specific, and immediate: Toast is acceptable or not. However, Harry has a number of other work expectations with respect to salt and pepper shakers, clearing and setting tables, and checking restrooms. These may distract and delay food service. Definitely a point for further investigation.

	Yes	No
2. Resources may be lacking (e.g., toasters, well-designed workspace) for servers to perform well.	☑	☐

From the information in this case, there appears to be only one toaster. This can lead to traffic jams, confusion as to whose toast is where, etc. The workspace around the toaster may be poorly designed. Definitely requires observation.

	Yes	No
3. Incentives and consequences are lacking for servers to perform well.	☐	☑

Very unlikely. The incentives for satisfactory service are tips. Consequences are size of tips, satisfied customers, and a satisfied Harry. Negative consequences are also clear, meaningful, and direct.

	Yes	No
4. Servers lack sufficient skills and knowledge to take toast orders, make toast, and serve toast correctly.	☐	☑

Once again, highly unlikely. Sure, there are subtleties to the bread slicing and some toaster adjustment is required. However, this is not brain surgery, and servers seem to be getting it right most of the time.

	Yes	No
5. Servers lack the capacity to make the toast correctly (e.g., physical/emotional/intellectual limitations).	☐	☑

Definitely not a factor here. As Harry says while observing new servers on their first day, "If they can't take the customer heat, then they stay out of the diner." Harry washes them out right away if they don't meet his demanding standards.

	Yes	No
6. Servers are not motivated to make and serve the toast correctly (e.g., do not value perfect toast, lack toast-making confidence, experience a negative mood about making and serving toast correctly).	☐	☑

Another definite no. Servers want to do the job right and reap the rewards for doing so. Harry's servers hate to disappoint customers, have no concerns about their abilities to make toast, and like the atmosphere and working conditions in the diner. (Don't let the 40 percent turnover rate fool you. That's very low in the diner business.)

Based on the Gilbert Model, we can draw three initial conclusions:

1. The main factors affecting performance appear to be environmental rather than individual.
2. Fixing the individual through training probably won't "fix the problem."

3. Eliminating or modifying non-serving-related expectations and improving toast-making resources (perhaps even redesigning the work space) might result in considerable performance improvement, probably at a lower cost than designing and running a training program.

Work, Workplace, Worker

Performance emerges from the interaction of three forces coming together:

- *Work*—what it is people have to do to achieve valued accomplishments. This includes work processes.
- *Workplace*—the environment in which the work is carried out. This includes not only the physical space and location, but also the cultural, emotional, administrative, and social dimensions. It also encompasses organizational structure and management success.
- *Worker*—the person who has to do the job, including characteristics, competencies, and caring about the job.

If any one of these is out of alignment, performance suffers. The Gilbert Model helps us focus on all of these. In the next chapter, you will encounter an operational model and set of steps that will help you analyze performance gaps *systematically* (in a step-by-step fashion) and *systemically* (maintaining a total, integrated view of all the elements affecting performance). You will also be able to identify causes of performance gaps; select suitable interventions; and then participate in the design, development, implementation, and monitoring of these interventions.

But first...

Remember This

A brief review of this chapter is in order. Please select the correct option in each of the following statements.

1. In general, workplace performance is more affected by (environmental/individual) factors.
2. Of the environmental factors affecting workplace performance, the category that is most frequently selected by workers is (information/resources/incentives and consequences).
3. Training, as an intervention to improve human performance, is most appropriate when workers lack (knowledge and skills/motivation).
4. The set of information factors that positively affects workplace performance includes (adequate tools, safe facilities/clear expectations, timely, specific feedback).

5. Rewards, recognition, and promotions are examples of (incentives and consequences/resources).

6. Amount of value attributed to a job, confidence to perform well, and mood fall into the (capacity/motivation) category of factors affecting performance.

7. "It is cheaper and easier to fix the (individual/environment)."

8. Performance emerges from the interaction of (training, technology, and tools/work, workplace, and worker).

And now for the feedback...

1. In general, workplace performance is more affected by environmental factors. The research suggests that 70 to 80 percent of workplace performance is affected by such variables as clarity of expectations, specificity and timeliness of feedback, adequacy of tools, materials and procedures, and appropriateness of incentives and consequences including opportunities for career advancement—all examples of environmental factors.

2. Of the environmental factors affecting workplace performance, the category that is most frequently selected by workers is information. Approximately 35 percent select the set of information factors compared with 26 percent for resources and 14 percent for incentives and consequences.

3. Training, as an intervention to improve human performance, is most appropriate when workers lack knowledge and skills. The purpose of all training efforts is to build competencies defined as the skills and knowledge required to perform job-specific tasks. Unfortunately, many organizations use training inappropriately when lack of performance requires other interventions.

4. The set of information factors that positively affects workplace performance includes clear expectations and timely, specific feedback. Adequate tools and safe facilities are also important, but fall into the resources set of factors.

5. Rewards, recognition, and promotion are examples of incentives and consequences. Applied appropriately, these can lead not only to desired performance but also to employee retention.

6. Amount of value attributed to a job, confidence to perform well, and mood fall into the motivation category of factors affecting performance. Motivation is frequently misunderstood, and lack of motivation is often cited as a major cause of poor performance. Motivation is, in fact, complex and made up of three key components: the amount of value attributed to a job, confidence to perform well, and mood. If any of the three are out of sync, motivation and, in turn, performance may suffer.

7. "It is cheaper and easier to fix the environment." Politically, it may require overcoming the obstacle of inertia—"We've always used training." However, the cost of designing, delivering, scheduling, and tracking training and its results, especially considering trainee salaries and lost opportunity, generally far exceeds the cost of environmental interventions. Creation of a job aid, streamlining of a procedure, or clarification of expectations and performance standards are relatively inexpensive means for improving people performance.

8. Performance emerges from the interaction of work, workplace, and worker. If the work is reasonable, appropriate, and clearly defined; the workplace is safe, well designed, and adequately resourced; and the workers are competent, confident, and caring, expect high performance. Deficiencies in any one of these leads to immediate decrease in performance—both behaviors and valued accomplishments.

At this point, the message should be very clear that training is rarely sufficient and often unnecessary to achieve desired performance improvement. The human performance system model and the Gilbert matrix have provided you with powerful lenses through which you can peer at and spot what needs to be done and what factors may have an impact on targeted human performance goals. What you are missing is a systematic methodology for attacking performance improvement projects. This is what the next chapter provides.

Chapter 5

Engineering Effective Performance

Chapter Highlights:

- ◆ A step-by-step methodology for closing performance gaps
- ◆ Engineering Effective Performance Model
- ◆ Seven techniques and tools for investigating factors affecting a performance gap
- ◆ A performance aid to help you identify potential interventions
- ◆ A matrix to assist you in selecting a workable set of interventions from those identified as potentials

Why Engineering?

Engineering seems like an odd, perhaps even threatening, term to use in speaking about the performance of people. It sounds like something out of a science fiction, mechanistic universe. However, if you take a step back, engineering is very appropriate given what it takes to organize all the conditions to achieve desired workplace results.

Engineering means designing or producing something by methods that have been derived from science and organized knowledge and by which the properties of matter and sources of energy are made useful to humans. How we achieve this usefulness can come from structure—how all the elements in a system are organized, from machines or from products in any practical combination or form. This is what you do when you engineer a performance system. You analyze; obtain resources; and then design, develop, test, implement, and monitor system activities and results.

Using the best data from a given situation and the knowledge gathered through study and experience in human performance improvement, this is what you should be able to do. And here is how you can do it.

An Operational-Procedural Model for Engineering Effective Performance

Figure 5-1 presents in graphic form our Engineering Effective Performance (EEP) Model. It is laid out in 10 steps. Please examine it slowly and carefully. Then read on, referring back to the figure from time to time to trace the flow.

Let's see how it all works. Along the way, if you haven't completely tired of Harry and his diner, we illustrate with this familiar example plus two others of a more corporate nature.

Steps in the EEP Process

STEP 1. IDENTIFY BUSINESS REQUIREMENTS

Your performance consulting responsibility, whether you have the title of performance consultant or fulfill the role, is to help your customers, colleagues, or organization achieve its performance mission—valued accomplishments—in the most cost-effective and efficient manner acceptable to all stakeholders. Unfortunately, only rarely does the true business requirement (or business need) arrive at your doorstep clearly articulated. Generally, you have to hunt for it.

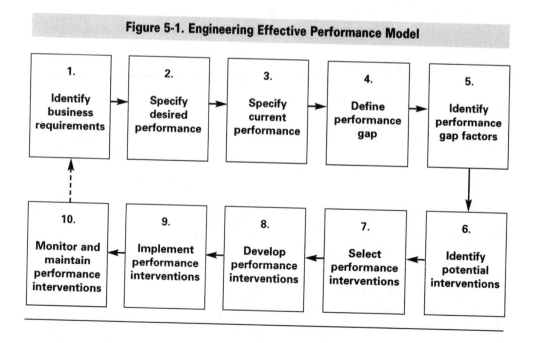

Figure 5-1. Engineering Effective Performance Model

The business requirement comes to you through two approaches:

- *Reactively*—someone approaches you with a request for help, often presented as training.
- *Proactively*—you are the initiator. Working with your clients and their organizations, you continuously scan the environment to identify business needs for which changes in people's performance will be necessary.

Here are several examples. Place an R beside reactive cases and a P beside proactive ones.

___ **1.** You notice escalating turnover rates in your call center.

___ **2.** Your customer mentions that safety violations have risen dramatically.

___ **3.** The Information Systems Director informs you that the new system will be implemented and that users will have to be trained on it.

___ **4.** The Regulatory Agency has imposed new requirements for handling dangerous goods, including four hours of training.

___ **5.** As you examine recent sales reports, you notice that sales personnel are not selling the higher-end printer models.

Here are the answers:

P for 1, 2, and 5, because in each case no one asked for help, you spotted an opportunity based on performance indicators: escalating turnover, rising safety violations, poor sales figures.

R for 3 and 4, because in these cases someone asked for an intervention or it was imposed by regulation and you are expected to respond—with training, of course.

Identifying the opportunity or receiving the request is only part of the activity in this step. You then have to probe and investigate to determine the business need. Sometimes it teases out fairly easily. Other times, you have to really press. Examine the following two scenarios.

Notice that in both cases, the first a proactive situation, the second a reactive one, the performance consultant had to probe to begin identifying the business need. What is your preliminary judgment in each case? Check your choice.

Lightning Electronics

PC (Performance Consultant): I just saw the latest sales reports, and I noticed that the Donner and Blitzen models aren't selling.

SM (Sales Manager): Yeah. Those higher-priced models sure are hard to move.

PC: Are they just too expensive for what they do?

SM: No. They're really good. Excellent speed, beautiful color, beat the pants off the competition. I really like their compact size and huge paper tray. We get great margins on them, too.

PC: So why aren't they selling?

SM: Well. The lower-end models are cheaper and make for a quicker sale. The sales staff aren't used to going after professionals and small business buyers. They'd rather push the low end because the commissions are about the same.

PC: Wouldn't you like to see the higher-end models sell more?

SM: Yeah. It sure would jack our revenues up and get us in closer with buyers that have a lot more to spend. It would be great.

Business need: Lightning Electronics case

- ☐ 1. **Increased sales, revenues; upscale market with more spending power**
- ☐ 2. **Better selling skills and greater knowledge of the products**

Pay Up

FSM (Financial Services Manager): We're installing a new payroll software system, and we'll need all our payroll clerks trained really well on it.

PC (Performance Consultant): I can help you solve this problem. Is the new system substantially different from the current one?

FSM: Quite different. We're moving to a Windows environment. The job will be the same, but the entries will be done very differently. We've started testing it, and the user interface is really ugly. Our initial tryouts show us that they'll be having a tough time.

PC: When you had the previous one installed, did payroll clerks have the same difficulties?

FSM: Oh yeah! We gave them training, but they still made lots of mistakes. We showed them how to do everything, but even today they use only about 20 to 30 percent of its capabilities.

PC: Should they be using more features?

FSM: For sure! But they don't. And they keep making the same errors over again. I hope your training does better with this new system. I'll tell you, we lose a lot of time and money dealing with payroll complaints. It affects morale and productivity too.

Business need: Pay Up case

- ☐ 1. **Better-trained payroll clerks who can use more features of the new system**
- ☐ 2. **Reduced costs associated with payroll, and improved employee morale and productivity due to reduced payroll errors**

In the first case, the answer is 1. In the second, 2. Both times, the performance consultant was able to help the customer articulate, even sketchily, where true business payoff lies. If you got the two cases correct, well done. You have gone beyond the superficial to touch the core. More probing will be required for you to finally expose the full business need.

STEP 2. SPECIFY DESIRED PERFORMANCE

Once you have identified the business requirements, you can zoom in on the desired performance outcomes. When working with your customers, one of the most effective techniques for achieving a starting point for this is to ask the following: "Imagine that your people are doing the job perfectly and that you and all other stakeholders, including the performers, are satisfied and delighted. What are they doing and achieving differently from what is currently happening?" Probe encouragingly to draw out all aspects of desired performance.

Case 1: Lightning Electronics

◆ The sales staff asks lots of open-ended questions to identify all the customers' needs, wants, and issues.
◆ Salespeople spot opportunities to demonstrate the value of the high-end printers compared with initial cost.
◆ Salespeople increase high-end printer sales.
◆ The sales teams are seeking out and obtaining more professional and small business customers with multiple higher-end needs.

Case 2: Pay Up

◆ Payroll clerks use the new system with no errors.
◆ Payroll clerks use a wide variety of system features to achieve complete, accurate, and timely results.
◆ Payroll complaints drop to zero.
◆ Employee morale and productivity increase due to excellent payroll procedures.
◆ The transition from the old to new system takes a very short time.

With these desired performance targets, some of them expressed as behaviors, others as accomplishments, you now have a clearer sense of direction as to what you should be delivering to your customer.

 Desired performance comes from three concerns:

◆ *Mandated or regulatory requirements.* Laws, regulations, company policy, certification requirements, or collective agreements may dictate not only desired performance, but even the means of achieving it (e.g., an eight-hour CPR class given by a state-certified trainer). Examine the requirements very carefully. Note whether an end result is mandated, such as passing a test or wearing appropriate gear, or the method is specified, such as three hours of training or taking a federally approved course. You will have to ensure that requirements are met as part of the interventions for achieving desired performance.

- *New system or product line introductions.* By system, we mean a new way of doing things, new products, new technologies, new culture and practices. It could also be something that already exists in the organization, but is new to the people who will be expected to deal with it. In most cases, if there is any level of complexity, some form of training is likely to be required, although it may not be in the form of courses. The expectation is that targeted performers will be able to perform well with the novelty.

- *Performance improvement.* This comes in two forms: opportunity and problem. Both are represented by a performance gap. An opportunity is a gap at the planning stage. A new goal or objective is set. You will have to help alter performance from its current—and possibly satisfactory—state to the new one. A problem is a gap at the control stage. Performers are not achieving at desired levels. In both cases, training, although perhaps necessary, is rarely sufficient as an intervention.

Specification of desired performance in clear, unambiguous terms sets the stage for the remaining steps. Identifying early on whether the source of the desired state is a mandate, a new system or product line introduction, a performance improvement, or any combination of these will help you in collecting detailed information and selecting interventions in later steps.

A final note on specifying desired performance. While your customer may be useful in describing the ideal state, he or she may not be sufficient. Other excellent sources include documentation, experts and consultants, management, customers, and the performers themselves.

STEP 3. SPECIFY CURRENT PERFORMANCE

Specification of current performance requires going to the source. Although your customer or other persons may be able to give you their observations and opinions, you really require hard data, such as:

- Sales figures
- Accident reports
- Productivity figures
- Revenues

- ◆ Record of complaints
- ◆ Work backlogs

- ◆ Grievances filed
- ◆ Error reports
- ◆ Customer satisfaction ratings

You would want to augment these data with supplementary quantitative information based on direct observation, surveys and questionnaires, interviews, focus groups, even performance tests you or an expert might administer. What guides you in your collection of current performance information is desired performance. If you have clearly specified what is desired, then what you are seeking is to compare the desired behaviors and accomplishments with current performance.

Returning to our Lightning Electronics case, we can see how this might work.

Lightning Electronics

Desired	Actual
• Sales staff ask a lot of open-ended questions to draw out all of the customer's needs, wants, and issues.	• 80 percent of questions are closed-ended; questions focus on the model customer is looking at or how much the customer wants to spend; 70 percent of the dialogue is sales responses to customer questions.
• Salespeople spot opportunities to demonstrate the value of the high-end printers compared with initial cost.	• Most sales interactions are transactional (i.e., How soon do you want it? Which computer will you connect it to?). Sales interaction focuses more on price than value; only 30 percent of sales staff compare printers; only 20 percent up-sell.
• Salespeople increase high-end printer sales.	• Percentage of high-end printer sales has not increased significantly over five quarters.
• The sales teams are targeting more professional and small business customers with multiple higher-end needs.	• More than 80 percent of sales are low-end home customers, mostly reactive sales. Higher-end customers obtained mostly by chance.

In a real situation, you would probably have more solid figures and hard data on both the desired and current sides.

STEP 4. DEFINE PERFORMANCE GAP

The harder your data in the previous steps, the more specific you can be here. There are three dimensions to a performance gap:

- ◆ *Magnitude*—how big and all-encompassing the gap is. Is the distance between desired and actual performance very wide? Is it prevalent organization-wide or simply local?

- *Value*—how much the gap represents to the organization in terms of revenues, profits, or cost savings.
- *Urgency*—how quickly it must be resolved. What are the consequences to the organization if not immediately handled?

Here is what a definition of the performance gap might look like in the Pay Up case.

Performance gap definition (Pay Up):

- **Magnitude**—all 600 payroll clerks, worldwide, are affected by the system change as well as, indirectly, all 45,000 company employees.

- **Value**—direct costs for investigating and correcting errors equal $1,170,000 to $1,755,000 annually (approximately 11,700 to 17,550 errors). Estimated value of impact on morale and productivity is 1 percent of total revenues, or $10,000,000, annually.

- **Urgency**—costly as this issue is, it also has an additional cascading effect on all workers and their supervisors. It reflects poorly on the company as a workplace of choice. Time to straighten out payroll issues, frustrations, hostilities, compounded errors, and, in some cases, family hardships resulting from errors get communicated among workers and cause negative ripple effects.

In summary, desired performance with the new system within six weeks of installation is 0 percent error rate with 100 percent on-time payroll entry and execution. Current performance is 1 to 1.5 percent error rate with associated direct and indirect costs detailed above, and 97 percent on-time entry and execution.

STEP 5. IDENTIFY PERFORMANCE GAP FACTORS

Factors affecting a performance gap fall into three categories:

- *Environmental*—These can be external such as changing market conditions, new competitive products, war, the availability of supplies, or more attractive job opportunities elsewhere. They may be internal and stem from organizational changes and pressures, from cultural issues—very frequent when mergers and acquisitions occur or there is a major senior management change—or from such job-specific factors as task interferences, inadequate tools and resources, poor incentives, lack of clearly expressed expectations, or insufficient feedback. Environmental factors are usually the most prevalent and have the most impact when there is a lack of desired performance compared to expectations.
- *Skill/knowledge*—These factors are related to lack of competencies to perform the job. The frequently cited test to determine if it is a lack of skills and knowledge that is the key set of factors to consider in a performance gap is: "If you put a gun to their head, can they perform as desired?"

While not a very pleasant question to ask, if the answer is "no," then lack of skills and/or knowledge is a definite factor for consideration.

◆ *Emotional/political*—This has to do with factors affecting motivation. These may stem from an overall negative workplace atmosphere—one filled with threats, general unhappiness with working conditions, perceived inequities, harassment, or insecurity about the future of the organization. They may also be highly specific and derive from supervisory practices, work cliques, or direct and indirect discriminatory or biased decision making.

Determining the factors and issues that must be dealt with to eliminate the gap between desired and actual is one of your most important tasks.

 Probably the contribution you can make that will have the most impact is to identify the key factors affecting a gap between desired and current performance. If you do this accurately, the appropriate course of action to achieve performance success emerges naturally.

 One of your critical roles is that of investigator and analyst. You mission is to track down and detail the performance gap factors.

How do you do this? By using a variety of techniques and tools. Table 5-1 lays out for you the most common ones performance consultants apply in hunting down factors affecting a specific performance gap. Examine the entries carefully. As you will immediately discover, there is no single means for discovering what you need to know. Almost every case requires a variety of techniques.

Also, as you examine the array of offerings in the table, bear in mind that you will be using these to discover—from a number of diverse sources—clarity about desired and actual performance; feelings about the gap; indications of causes for the gap if this is a performance improvement issue; barriers to achieving desired performance; and what might constitute viable, cost-effective solutions as well as unworkable ones.

Although other methods for gathering information exist, these in the table are the ones most frequently used.

To close out on this very important step for engineering effective performance, imagine that you would like to investigate and gather information at Harry's Diner to identify factors affecting the performance gap. Using Worksheet 5-1, select the techniques you think you would apply in this case. Also select your source of information.

Table 5-1. Techniques and Tools for Investigating Factors Affecting a Performance Gap

Technique/ Tool	Advantages	Disadvantages	Sources/Targets
Existing data analysis	• Already available • Factual • Highly credible • Generally easy to obtain • Generally easy to investigate and report	• May require authorizations and/or technical assistance • Static, inert, requires interpretation • Subject to multiple interpretations • Often lacks context	• Exemplary performance data • Benchmark data • Research study data • Sales figures • Accident/incident report figures • Complaint/callback logs • Work backlog data • Productivity figures • Revenues • Grievance reports • Error logs • Absentee data • Wastage data
Documentation analysis	• Already available • Accessible in hard/soft copy formats • Specific and detailed • Can be referred to repeatedly • Does not require scheduling to access	• Time consuming to locate, sort, and review • Requires a lot of time for study • Static and impersonal—cannot be probed • Requires considerable time to synthesize	• Research reports • Productivity reports • Company manuals • Company reports • Books • Journal articles • Examples from other departments/organizations • Industry/government reports • Grievance files • Performance reports • Minutes of meetings • Standard operating procedures and official bulletins
Surveys and questionnaires	• Large samples • Quick to distribute and administer • Easy to tabulate and synthesize	• Generally very low response rates • Difficult to create clear, unambiguous items • Provides relatively superficial and often subjective data	• Experts • Managers/supervisors • Customers • Targeted performers • Groups outside the organization facing similar issues • Benchmark organizations
Observation	• Directly acquired data at the source • Credible • Relatively easy to tabulate and report	• Requires observer training • Costly and time consuming • Not always feasible • People act differently when observed • Unless sampled broadly and at different times, may not reflect general situation	• Targeted performers • Supervisors • Customer reactions • Work transactions • Meetings

Technique/ Tool	Advantages	Disadvantages	Sources/Targets
Structured interviews	• Generally easy to construct • Permits delving deeply • Detailed and rich • Allows for probing • Adds context and color	• Costly and time consuming to conduct • Requires some interviewer training and practice • Bias and subjectivity can intrude in questioning and responses • Difficult to analyze and synthesize	• Management • Experts • Customers • Supervisors • Targeted performers • Peers of targeted performers • Former performers • New hires prior to job entry • Performers quitting the job or organization
Focus group	• Efficient compared with interviews • Permits delving deeply • Generates synergy among participants	• Scheduling of seven to 10 participants simultaneously • Subjectivity in questioning and responding • Group think (effect of a strong leader) • Difficult to analyze, synthesize, and report results of several groups	• Management • Customers • Targeted performers • Supervisors • Experts • Former performers
Performance testing	• Provides hard data • Controlled conditions • Reflects actual performance, credible	• Can create test anxiety • Demands test validity • Can be costly and time consuming • Could incite negative reactions in workers	• Targeted performers • Potential job hires

Check off your selections on pages 58 and 59. You can select more than one source for each technique you choose. Be realistic. You're helping your brother-in-law . . . and this is a diner.

Then, come back and compare those items you checked off with what we feel is appropriate. We warn you in advance: There is no correct answer. This is our best guess:

- *Existing data analysis*—wastage data. We might find it useful to verify exactly when and why waste increases at certain periods.
- *Observation*—targeted performers, customer reactions, work transactions. It would be useful to observe the entire order, slicing, toast-making, pickup, and delivery process to spot problems and weaknesses as well as how rejections and rework are handled.

Worksheet 5-1. Techniques and Tools for Investigating Factors Affecting a Performance Gap—Harry's Diner

Technique	Source
☐ Existing data analysis	☐ Exemplary performance data ☐ Benchmark data ☐ Research study data ☐ Sales figures ☐ Accident/incident report figures ☐ Complaint/callback logs ☐ Work backlog data ☐ Productivity figures ☐ Revenues ☐ Grievance reports ☐ Error logs ☐ Absentee data ☐ Wastage data
☐ Documentation analysis	☐ Research reports ☐ Productivity reports ☐ Company manuals ☐ Company reports ☐ Books ☐ Journal articles ☐ Examples from other departments/ organizations ☐ Industry/government reports ☐ Grievance files ☐ Performance reports ☐ Minutes of meetings ☐ Standard operating procedures and official bulletins
☐ Surveys and questionnaires	☐ Management ☐ Customers ☐ Supervisors ☐ Targeted performers
☐ Observation	☐ Targeted performers ☐ Supervisors ☐ Customer reactions ☐ Work transactions ☐ Meetings

Technique	Source
☐ Structured interviews	☐ Management ☐ Experts ☐ Customers ☐ Supervisors ☐ Targeted performers ☐ Peers of targeted performers ☐ Former performers ☐ New hires prior to job entry ☐ Performers quitting the job or organization
☐ Focus groups	☐ Management ☐ Customers ☐ Targeted performers ☐ Supervisors ☐ Experts ☐ Former performers
☐ Performance testing	☐ Targeted performers ☐ Potential job hires

- *Structured interviews*—management (Harry), customers (small sample), targeted performers. Interviewing Harry helps clarify his concerns, resources, limitations, and expectations as well as feelings. Customer interviews allow us to understand their reactions, level of frustration or understanding and loyalty to Harry's Diner, and their perception of the situation. These will also help you to obtain potentially valuable suggestions from experienced customers. Server interviews would enlighten you on their perceptions and experience with the process. They would also provide you with front-line suggestions for improvement.
- *Focus groups*—targeted performers (servers). Pulling together a small group of servers after the rush (between breakfast and lunch) or at the start of the day may generate some excellent observations and suggestions. If these are later applied, the servers may sense ownership of the changes, which can generate a positive impact on performance.

We used Harry's Diner for you to practice step 5. You might wish to stop for a moment and imagine which techniques and tools you would select for the Lightning Electronics and Pay Up cases.

Remember. There is no perfect set of investigative tools. Time, resources, feasibility, as well as appropriateness will guide your choices. Credibility in reporting is also an important consideration.

STEP 6. IDENTIFY POTENTIAL INTERVENTIONS

There are three key points to retain in identifying potential interventions. First, the better you execute step 5, identify performance gap factors, the easier it is to identify the relevant interventions. This makes good sense. If feedback is lacking, what's the obvious intervention? The same holds true if you have identified uncertainty, dissatisfaction, and fear resulting from a recent merger as having a major impact on performers. Or lack of proper tools. Your main job in this step is to list the factors affecting performance—supported by data from your findings—and then line them up with obvious and logical intervention solutions. Shortly, you'll get a chance to try this out.

The second point is that there is a limitless array of possible interventions. A sampling of interventions is listed below.

• Additional resources	• Improved information access	• Process reengineering
• Career development plans	• Incentive systems	• Reference materials
• Coaching	• Increased encouragement	• Removal of administrative obstacles
• Culture change	• Increased supervision	
• Electronic performance support tools and systems	• Improved standards	• Selection systems
• Elimination of interfering tasks	• Job aids	• Structured on-the-job training programs
• Environmental design	• Leadership programs	• Team building
• Ergonomics	• Motivational systems	• Training
• Feedback systems	• Organizational redesign	• Wellness programs
	• Performance management systems	

Don't fear, however. Most performance gaps can be decreased or eliminated by applying a more manageable set of interventions. We will provide you with a performance aid a little further on to help you with this process.

Third point. You identify interventions. You don't necessarily have to follow through with actually developing these yourself. This is very important. Think of Harry's Diner. Let's say that you identify a lack of resources as one of the factors affecting performance. In other words, one toaster is not enough. Your obvious recommendation for Harry's Diner is to purchase and install another toaster. Who does this? Make your choice.

☐ **You**
☐ **Harry**

Our choice is definitely Harry or one of his people. What do you know about commercial toasters? Selecting and installing the new additional toaster is beyond the performance consultant's repertoire of knowledge and skills. You can assist Harry or even help find a suitable resource. However, you are not required to execute. In a future chapter, we'll deal with your specific areas of responsibility.

We now turn to a tool to help you identify potential interventions: Worksheet 5-2 on selection of performance interventions.

Worksheet 5-2. Performance Intervention Selection

Based on the data collected in the previous steps, identify potential interventions as follows:

If the data indicate that performers...	Then check off as a potential intervention...	
Lack skills and/or knowledge essential for the job	Training	☐
Lack job-relevant skills and knowledge or perform too slowly or make errors but could do the job at desired levels if they had readily accessible information, procedures, decision tables, or information systems and tools	Job aids	☐
Lack clear expectations of how they should perform	Setting specific, clear performance expectations	☐
Lack clear and specific standards of performance	Setting performance standards	☐
Lack timely, specific information on how they are performing	Feedback systems	☐
Lack appropriate prerequisite skills, knowledge, background, or personal characteristics and/or values to rapidly meet performance requirements	Selection systems	☐
Face interferences that discourage or prevent desired performance	Elimination of task interferences	☐
Have to work outside of the prescribed way the job has been structured to achieve desired performance requirements	Job redesign	☐

(continued on page 62)

Worksheet 5-2. Performance Intervention Selection (continued)

If the data indicate that performers...	Then check off as a potential intervention...	
Face organizational obstacles (structural, communications, climate, administrative, infrastructural) that inhibit performance	Organizational redesign	☐
Face physical obstacles or dangers that inhibit performance	Environmental redesign	☐
Work with inefficient processes that inhibit desired performance	Process redesign	☐
Are not meaningfully encouraged or rewarded or are even punished for desired performance or do not perceive the reward system as fair and equitable	Incentives/consequences systems	☐
Do not value desired performance, do not feel confident they can perform, or do not feel challenged to perform	Motivation systems	☐
Lack required tools, time, supplies, or support systems	Provision of resources	☐
Lack access to information necessary to perform	Provision of information	☐
Are not encouraged or supported by supervisors or management	Increased management support	☐
Are not supported by appropriate specialists	Increased technical support	☐
Are faced with a major change in the way the job is done or the organization functions	Change management support and strategies	☐
_____	_____	
_____	_____	

Add to the left-hand column other factors that you discover affecting the performance gap. In the right-hand column, list appropriate interventions.

 Most performance gaps have more than one cause and, hence, more than one solution. Check off all the potential interventions. Don't worry if there are many. In the next step, you'll reduce these to a workable number.

Now, let's put this performance aid to work. You have not had a real chance to apply all of your data-gathering tools and techniques to any of our three cases: Harry's

Diner, Lightning Electronics, Pay Up. Nevertheless, imagine that you had actually gone out and observed, interviewed, run a focus group, and reviewed data on toast wastage at Harry's Diner. What do you think you might have discovered? Go back to Worksheet 5-2 and review each of the items in the left-hand column. Then check off those interventions in the right-hand column that you consider potentially appropriate. Use your imagination. We know you have insufficient data. The purpose is to try out the performance aid. Once you have finished, let's compare responses.

We actually know Harry's Diner. Based on our real data collection, here is what we checked off:

- Elimination of task interferences
- Job redesign (may have to change tasks)
- Environmental redesign (they bunch up in one location)
- Process redesign (they don't always write down orders)
- Provision of resources (another toaster).

We have done this exercise with workshop participants who generally come close to our list. We suspect you have too. We didn't retain the other options for the following reasons:

- **Training:** They know how to slice the bread, make the toast, etc.
- **Job aids:** Seven different kinds of bread and each customer custom-ordering slices. Forget it!
- **Performance expectations:** These are clear from the customers and Harry.
- **Performance standards:** Ditto.
- **Timely information on performance:** Immediate and direct from customers.
- **Prerequisites, characteristics, and values:** Harry selects with an experienced eye and weeds out those who don't cut it.
- **Organizational obstacles:** Not relevant.
- **Not meaningfully rewarded:** Perfect toast results in better tips.
- **Value desired performance:** Servers want to do well. It's not fun facing dissatisfied customers.
- **Lack access to necessary information:** Customer orders are clear.
- **Not encouraged by management:** On the contrary. Harry really is there to encourage and support accurate, timely orders.
- **Not supported by specialists:** Hey! We're talking about making toast.
- **Change management support and strategies:** This is not a major change that negatively affects anyone. In fact, the changes should make things move more smoothly.

Table 5-2. Potential Interventions: Lightning Electronics and Pay Up

Lightning Electronics	Pay Up
• Training	• Training
• Job aids	• Job aids
• Setting performance expectations	• Setting performance standards
• Feedback systems	• Feedback systems
• Incentives/consequences	• Process redesign
• Motivational systems	• Provisions of resources*
• Increased management support	• Increased technical support*
• Change management support and strategies	• Change management support and strategies

* Something will have to be done to the ugly interface. Either the interface must be changed or, if impossible to do so, resources to deal with it will be required.

To end discussion on step 6, Table 5-2 presents what the data might indicate as potential interventions for the Lightning Electronics and Pay Up cases.

At this point, you may be shaking your head and worriedly groaning, "All of these!" Yes, all of these are factors to consider. Take heart, however. The next step will help you make some hard-nosed, reality-based decisions.

STEP 7. SELECT PERFORMANCE INTERVENTIONS

There is a huge difference between "identify" and "select." In this step, you lay out all the potential interventions, apply four criteria, and make your selection. Ideally, it would be wonderful to do it all. In reality, as you know only too well, you must make choices. And the choices are significant, because with each choice you let go, you increase the risk of not completely eliminating the gap.

 Before you begin making choices, here is an important point to bear in mind. Your list of potential interventions may, at first appearance, seem long. Consider that some of the interventions do not require a tremendous amount of effort. Clarifying expectations, increasing supervisory support, or eliminating interfering tasks, for example, may simply be resolved through a few meetings and a cleaning up of existing practices. On the other hand, a single intervention such as training may demand a huge amount of resources and time. So, don't worry about the number of potential interventions . . . yet. Instead, focus on the following four criteria: appropriateness, economics, feasibility, and acceptability.

- *Appropriateness.* This criterion is the most important. Examine each intervention. Decide, based on the data, how suitable it is with respect to closing the gap between "is" and "should be." The more essentially appropriate the intervention is, the greater the likelihood of your retaining it.

- *Economics.* The intervention may be a great one, but can the organization afford it? You have to examine your budgets and all available financial resources. Money, sadly, is a major consideration.

- *Feasibility.* This criterion asks you the following: "Given your timelines, resources, and constraints, can you do it?" Even if money is no object and the fit is great, the time constraints, your capabilities, or a lack of resources may simply not support the intervention.

- *Acceptability.* There are two dimensions to this criterion: organizational and performer. Any intervention you select must fit with the organizational culture and norms. It has to be coherent with current practices and organizational image. There are times when an innovative intervention is worthwhile implementing despite the fact that it goes counter to the organizational grain. These instances are rare, however, and must be well founded and supported if they are to work. For the most part, organizational compatibility is a major consideration.

  The same holds true for the targeted performers. Any intervention you select must be acceptable to them. You may have to build convincing arguments to demonstrate value. However, if the intervention is not acceptable to the workers who must live with it, then the probabilities of its success greatly diminish.

How do you put this all together? Very simply. In a two-dimensional matrix, you lay out the identified solutions from step 6 along the vertical axis and the four selection criteria along the horizontal, as in Worksheet 5-3.

Notice that you have columns for a total, a rank, and for checking off your final selections.

Now, the scoring system. For each criterion, you score each intervention as follows:

   4 = Perfect fit. No problem.
   3 = Good fit. We can make it work.
   2 = OK fit. Not a great choice. We will have to stretch.
   1 = Poor fit. This will require a lot of effort. Probably should not do it.
   0 = Cannot be done. Eliminate this intervention.

Note: a single "0" for any criterion automatically eliminates the intervention.

Worksheet 5-3. The Basics of a Performance Intervention Selection Matrix

Interventions	Selection criteria				Total	Rank	Retain (✓)
	Appropriateness	Economics	Feasibility	Acceptability			

Once you have scored each intervention for all four criteria, total the scores and rank order them. Eliminate any with a "0." Retain the highest-ranked interventions. The cutoff will depend on your organization's circumstances. Hold onto the interventions you cut off for later examination. Sometimes you have to make progress in small steps.

Worksheet 5-4 shows you how you might score the intervention for Harry's Diner. You will have to work with Harry and other team members to come to consensus on scores. Client input is essential.

Based on discussions and negotiations with Harry and the servers, three interventions are retained. A new toaster will be purchased; certain server tasks will be passed over to the runners (bussers); and the order-taking, toast-making, toast-delivery process will be reexamined to improve service efficiencies and effectiveness. Job redesign may come later. At this point, changing around the diner's environment is unacceptable to Harry.

Worksheets 5-5 and 5-6 provide two more examples based on our previous cases.

In the Lightning Electronics case, management has agreed to virtually everything, as the benefits of up-selling are evident to all. Temporarily, bonuses will be given for meeting and exceeding performance expectations. Later, the commission structure will be reassessed. Because management doesn't understand "change management," this intervention will be deferred for now.

In the Pay Up case, through tough negotiations and really examining the data, management has accepted and will support all recommendations except for feedback, resources, and change management. Too many decisions about the new software were made without examining the "people" factor. As a result, budgets are exhausted. Management will provide global feedback to payroll clerks. No changes to the interface will be made at this late date. Change management will only be conducted on an ad hoc basis. Supervisors will receive some training on this.

Not all tales end happily. What we can glean from the three examples is that the constraints of an organization play a major role in the final intervention selection. What also occurs is an educational side effect. The way you conduct the first seven steps of the EEP Model not only helps in determining what interventions will work, but also educates clients and management about what it takes to obtain desired performance. This is extremely beneficial—often more so than the impact on the current project.

STEP 8. DEVELOP PERFORMANCE INTERVENTIONS

The explanation for this step and the next two will be less detailed than the first seven. The reason is simple. Engineering effective performance is highly

Worksheet 5-4. Performance Intervention Selection: Harry's Diner

Interventions	Selection criteria				Total	Rank	Retain (✓)
	Appropriateness	Economics	Feasibility	Acceptability			
Elimination of task interferences	4	3	2	3	12	3	✓
Job redesign	3	1	1	3	8	4	
Environmental redesign	3	0	0	2	5	5	
Process redesign	4	4	3	3	14	2	✓
Provision of resources	4	3	4	4	15	1	✓

Worksheet 5-5. Performance Intervention Selection: Lightning Electronics

Interventions	Selection criteria				Total	Rank	Retain (✓)
	Appropriateness	Economics	Feasibility	Acceptability			
Training	4	3	3	3	13	3	✓
Job aids	4	4	4	4	16	1	✓
Performance expectations	4	4	4	3	15	2	✓
Feedback	4	2	2	4	12	6	✓
Incentives/ Consequences	4	2	2	3	11	7	✓
Motivation	3	4	4	2	13	3	✓
Management support	4	3	3	2	12	3	✓
Change management	3	2	2	2	9	8	

Worksheet 5-6. Performance Intervention Selection: Pay Up

Interventions	Selection criteria				Total	Rank	Retain (✓)
	Appropriateness	Economics	Feasibility	Acceptability			
Training	4	3	4	4	15	2	✓
Job aids	4	4	4	4	16	1	✓
Performance standards	4	4	4	2	14	3	✓
Feedback	4	2	1	2	9	5	
Process redesign	4	2	3	2	11	4	✓
Resources	4	0	0	2	6	6	
Technical support	3	2	1	3	9	5	✓
Change management	4	2	2	1	9	5	

dependent on your identifying and diagnosing performance gaps and then working with your clients to select the interventions that will work. Once the basket of interventions has been determined, your role as an active participant may decrease. Each intervention requires its own design and development team. You can play a variety of roles in supporting efforts. These will be presented in detail in the next chapter.

In step 8, developing the performance interventions requires three major steps: design, creation, and verification.

Design

Whether the intervention is training, job aids, process redesign, or a new incentive system, each must be initially designed. The first five steps of the EEP Model provide the basis for each design. In step 8, additional analytic work will be required to determine which design will fit best for each intervention. For training, there is a whole process known as instructional systems design (ISD), which lays out a roadmap for building sound skill and knowledge interventions. Similarly, other roadmaps exist for many of the other interventions (e.g., process redesign, feedback systems, incentive systems). The For Further Reading section of this book offers you some excellent titles to explore.

Creation

The design is the important step. It generally includes specifications for developing the intervention. Depending on the nature of the intervention, this creation phase may be performed by you or by others. You may be highly qualified to develop training and job aids and can work with clients to create clear expectations, means for management support or feedback, and motivational systems. For interventions such as process or environmental redesign or the development of incentive systems, you are likely to require specialists. The result of the creation phase is a prototype of each intervention, ready for expert verification and tryout.

Worksheet 5-7 provides a list of intervention categories. Take a moment to conduct a self-assessment with respect to your ability to design and create performance interventions. Check off what you consider to be the appropriate response for yourself. You will notice that there are options to learn how to do these or to pass it on to others—perfectly acceptable alternatives.

The EEP Model is based on the concept of teamwork. No one can do it all. Every step requires others to support you or work with you as partners. In steps 8, 9, and 10, it is likely that you will frequently be playing the support role.

Worksheet 5-7. Self-Assessment for Designing and Creating Performance Interventions

Interventions	Design			Creation		
	I can do it (✓)	I should learn how to do it (✓)	Someone else should do it (✓)	I can do it (✓)	I should learn how to do it (✓)	Someone else should do it (✓)
Training						
Job aids						
Setting specific, clear performance expectations						
Feedback systems selection						
Elimination of task interferences						
Job redesign						
Organizational redesign						
Environmental redesign						
Process redesign						
Incentives/ consequences systems						
Motivation systems						
Provision of resources						
Increased management support						
Increased technical support						
Change management support and strategies						

Verification

Once you have an intervention or set of interventions in prototype form, you ensure that they are validated and tested. The purpose is to verify that each intervention is sound from the content, management, and legal perspective and that it will produce desired results once implemented.

STEP 9. IMPLEMENT PERFORMANCE INTERVENTIONS

The tried and true adage of "If you fail to plan, you plan to fail" is particularly relevant in the implementation step of the EEP Model. You have invested so much effort to analyze the performance gap; identify and select suitable interventions; and design, create, and test these, it would be a shame if all went to waste due to poor implementation.

The implementation step can be broken down into three main phases: planning, execution, and support.

Planning

Implementation planning begins long before you arrive at step 9. During the analysis steps, you collect a great deal of information not only about the gap, but also the context, the performers, the resources, and the constraints of the situation. Once you have selected your basket of performance interventions (step 7), you begin to plan implementation in earnest. An effective approach is to lay out a time and action (or task) calendar, listing everything that needs to be done, who is responsible for its happening, what obstacles or problems might occur, and potential solutions for overcoming these. A simple implementation planning sheet partially filled in for the Lightning Electronics case is presented in Worksheet 5-8.

Track all tasks, inserting completion dates and adding new tasks as necessary.

Execution

Little things mean a lot. Friendly invitations to events, excellent materials ready and waiting, incentive and feedback systems operational, even hot coffee and refreshments all have to be in a "go" mode. Implementation requires checking on every detail. Creating checklists such as the one shown in Worksheet 5-9 may appear overly compulsive. Our experience has taught us that this is not the case. You know that anything that can go wrong often does. Beat the odds through fastidious execution of your interventions. The result is a higher probability of performance success.

Support

Implementation of any set of performance improvement interventions requires two types of support: for the implementation of the interventions themselves and for the targeted performers. Let's examine each of these.

Worksheet 5-8. Implementation Planning Sheet: Lightning Electronics

Project: High-End Printer Sales

Client contact: Chad Kandaswami (7-7321)

Implementation target date: October 31

Task	Person responsible	Date due	Potential problems/ obstacles	Potential solutions	Date task completed
Schedule training room	Debra G.	08/15	• Other conflicting events	• Negotiate with other events planners • Book hotel rooms	
Print training materials and job aids	Raj S.	10/25	• Masters not ready	• Warn developers of drop-dead dates • Monitor • Get additional help	
Initiate bonus systems	Iriana G.	10/15	• Missing final approvals • Accounting systems not ready	• Get Chad K. to obtain signatures at management meeting • See Mel J. in Finance; work closely with the payroll group	
Set managers meeting date on feedback and support	Debra G.	09/15	• Managers don't see this as a priority and may not show up	• Get Claudia M. (EVP) to write a "must" note to managers • Contact all managers and get commitment to meeting	
Get full line of high-end printers for training sessions along with customer profiles	Raj S.	08/07 09/07	• Availability of all machines • Lack of tech support	• Get Chad K. to obtain commitment in writing from Distribution • See Olaf P. to commit a tech support person for training sessions	

Worksheet 5-9. Implementation Checklist: Lightning Electronics

Training

- Trainers selected ☐
- Trainers notified ☐
- All materials printed ☐
- Evaluation tools completed ☐
- Rooms reserved ☐
- Rooms prepared ☐
- Equipment verified ☐
- Printers ordered ☐
- Printers delivered ☐
- Security verified ☐
- Tech support scheduled ☐
- Trainers trained ☐
- Supplies ordered ☐
- Supplies received ☐
- Reference guide ordered ☐
- Reference guide received ☐
- Interfering events handled ☐
- Refreshments arranged ☐

Feedback (FB)

- FB system approved ☐
- FB system installed ☐
- FB system communicated to:
  - Sales associates ☐
  - Sales managers ☐
  - Senior managers ☐

Motivation

- Sample cases prepared ☐
- Sample cases printed ☐
- Sample cases distributed ☐
- Initiative value proposition distributed:
  - Sales associates ☐
  - Sales managers ☐

Job Aids

- Job aids printed ☐
- Job aids packaged ☐

Performance Expectations

- Expectations approved ☐
- Expectations printed ☐
- Expectations distributed ☐
- Receipt of expectations verified:
  - Sales associates ☐
  - Sales managers ☐

Management Support

- EVP sales letter written ☐
- EVP sales letter printed ☐
- EVP sales letter distributed ☐
- Manager meetings scheduled ☐
- Manager calendars cleared ☐
- Meeting agenda set ☐
- Support job aids developed ☐
- Support job aids printed ☐
- Tracking system developed ☐

Incentives

- Incentive system approved ☐
- Incentive rules printed ☐
- Incentive system communicated to:
  - Sales associates ☐
  - Sales managers ☐
  - Senior managers ☐
- Accounting/payroll systems prepared ☐

You are initiating a number of interventions at once or perhaps in a phased approach. To ensure that all you have worked for is perceived as valuable, credible, doable, and sustainable, you will have to find champions and supporters. These will help you find resources, enroll targeted workers, ensure participation, and generally act as cheerleaders. Without this type of enthusiastic support, probabilities of performance change and success decrease. As you build your interventions, build your support team:

- Senior champions to lend weight to the cause.
- Informal leaders to increase credibility.
- Supervisors to ensure commitment, engagement, and perseverance.
- Other groups and individuals to make sure implementation runs smoothly. These may include administrative personnel who send out notices and gather supplies, technical support specialists who ensure systems and tools work, public relations specialists who publicize the project, even caterers to keep refreshments going as needed.

Implementation support also includes the preparation, encouragement, and monitoring of performance once the interventions are launched. The key persons in this are the first-line supervisors. Enroll them in the cause. Demonstrate value to them. Provide training and support to them so that they, in turn, can support you—and, more important, the people who report to them.

Let's take a moment to snoop into some implementation breakdowns. In which phase of implementation was there an omission? Circle the P if you think it was in the planning, E in the execution, or S if it was in support.

Implementation breakdown:	Probably in phase:		
1. The interventions, including training, were ready, but no meeting space was available.	P	E	S
2. Performance bonuses were paid erratically even though the systems were checked out beforehand.	P	E	S
3. "If the boss doesn't seem to care, why should I?"	P	E	S
4. Some of the printers didn't work, and there was nobody available to fix them when we called tech support.	P	E	S
5. The supervisors were all ready, primed, and excited about prepping their teams, but they didn't have tools or guidance to support their enthusiasm and efforts.	P	E	S

Here are our responses:

1. P—This is a planning glitch. Someone forgot to reserve the required facilities in advance.
2. E—The planning worked, but obviously the systems hadn't been fully checked out.
3. S—It appears as though the "boss" was not recruited and prepared to support the performance intervention effort.
4. P—The implementation planning failed to include technical support—a big mistake when dealing with products and technologies.
5. E—It looks as though this is an execution issue. The supervisors appear to have been prepared and are supportive. Somehow, written guidelines to help them were not included. (If you selected P, you can definitely make a good case for this choice too.)

In summary, implementation is a critical consideration in any performance enhancement initiative, no matter how small. It starts earlier than step 9, but then becomes increasingly more important as you proceed to launch.

STEP 10. MONITOR AND MAINTAIN PERFORMANCE INTERVENTIONS

There is a whole lifecycle to performance improvement. It may begin with gap identification and progress to intervention development and implementation, but nothing ever stands still in our frenetic, modern-day workplaces. Once implemented, you must constantly monitor performance to verify that it is indeed improving. You also have to monitor business results, which were the initial drivers for all of your efforts. To monitor, you must establish valid metrics both for performance and for business results. The two key questions you should continually ask are: "Are people performing as desired?" and "Are we getting the valued accomplishments the business has targeted?" A "no" to either of these requires further investigation, corrective action, and additional monitoring.

It seems as though a performance consultant's work is never done. True. This is both good and bad news. Choose which one you prefer to read about—or read both in the box on page 78.

Good news or bad, everything comes down to implementation, monitoring, and maintenance. Your role never ends. We think this is . . . great!

EEP Summary

Please don't be overwhelmed by the EEP Model and all the steps and tasks for improving performance. It sounds like a lot. And you may, at this point, be saying

A Performance Consultant's Work is Never Done . . .

Good News	Bad News
• There's always work for you. Performance improvement is ongoing and continuous. The exciting challenge is in trying to eliminate that gap.	• It never ends. You barely have time to breathe before new gaps present themselves.
• Once a gap has been reduced or eliminated, you have demonstrated your worth. Your increased credibility means more people recognize your value to the organization.	• Pressure is constant to maintain one performance system while starting on new, demanding performance improvement projects. And as soon as the ball is dropped, performance begins to decline.
• Constant new challenges offer continual opportunities for learning and professional growth.	• Nothing stays the same. By implementation time, some of the gap factors may have changed. Who has time to get back to the drawing board?
	• Once implementation occurs, the power and control shifts to the client, managers, supervisors, unions, and workers. You may have developed a wonderful package of performance improvement interventions, but the success depends on others.

"I think I'll just focus on training." Stop. Training simply ain't performance. Believing it is will not change what many years tell us about workplace performance. Once you shift your thinking away from training order-taker to that of performance consultant, you will see not only the benefits of applying the EEP Model, but you'll also enjoy your enhanced role.

 Remember This

As usual, we conclude this lengthy chapter with a review. Select in each of the following statements the alternative you believe fits best. Feedback immediately follows.

1. Engineering means designing or producing by methods derived from (science and organized knowledge/logic and creative problem solving) to achieve practical results.

2. As a professional focused on meeting your clients' business needs, your prime mission is to achieve valued (learning/performance) results.

3. As a performance consultant, when a client brings you a request—reactive mode—you must probe to identify the underlying business need. This is (also true/not true) in the proactive mode.

4. Desired performance comes from three fundamental business concerns. These are (meeting mandatory or regulatory requirements/increasing workers'

knowledge and skills/rapidly getting up to speed with new products or systems/a need for improved performance to meet business goals).

5. An opportunity is a gap at the (control/planning) stage; a problem is a gap at the (control/planning) stage.

6. What guides you in your collecting of current performance information is (what your customer recommends as useful/desired performance).

7. Magnitude, value, and urgency are three dimensions of a (performance intervention/performance gap).

8. Use of e-learning or a blended learning strategy is potentially (appropriate/inappropriate) for overcoming skill and knowledge deficiencies.

9. If performers are not meaningfully encouraged or rewarded for desired performance, an appropriate intervention would be (a fair and equitable incentive system/job aids to facilitate performance).

10. "If you fail to plan, you plan to fail" is a key principle of the (implementation/monitoring and maintenance) step of the EEP Model.

Our selections:

1. Engineering means designing or producing by methods derived from science and organized knowledge to achieve practical results. Engineering is a form of technology. It draws from what science has discovered and from solid professional experience to create systems—interventions—that benefit humans. Logic and creative problem solving are mental processes used in engineering.

2. As a professional focused on meeting your clients' business needs, your prime mission is to achieve valued performance results. Learning may be a means of achieving the performance results, but it is not the end—the client's ultimate success criterion.

3. As a performance consultant, when a client brings you a request—reactive mode—you must probe to identify the underlying business need. This is also true in the proactive mode. You may spot what you perceive is a gap. Probing brings it into sharper focus and helps tease out that true business need.

4. Desired performance comes from three fundamental business concerns. These are meeting mandatory or regulatory requirements, rapidly getting up to speed with new products or systems, and a need for improved performance to meet business goals. Increasing workers' knowledge and skills may be a means for meeting any of these three fundamental business concerns.

5. An opportunity is a gap at the planning stage; a problem is a gap at the control stage. No commentary required.

6. What guides you in your collecting of current performance information is desired performance. Desired performance sets the bar. Once this has been specified, you examine current performance with respect to it to define the gap. Your customer can help in this process, but it is the desired set of behaviors and valued accomplishments that act as a beacon for studying current performance.

7. Magnitude, value, and urgency are three dimensions of a performance gap. They characterize the distance between desired and actual performance.

8. Use of e-learning or a blended learning strategy is potentially appropriate for overcoming skill and knowledge deficiencies. Learning solutions of any kind may be considered to improve skills and knowledge.

9. If performers are not meaningfully encouraged or rewarded for desired performance, an appropriate intervention would be a fair and equitable incentive system. Research studies clearly demonstrate that incentives perceived as fair and equitable improve performance when skills and knowledge, resources, and required information are present. Job aids help to overcome skill and knowledge gaps by acting as external performance guides or means for presenting required information.

10. "If you fail to plan, you plan to fail" is a key principle of the implementation step of the EEP Model. It is probably appropriate throughout the entire model, but is key to implementation—and the earlier the planning begins, the better!

What a journey you have taken in this chapter. Ten steps, numerous principles, procedures, and performance aids. But what a great journey! You have traversed along a pathway to successful engineering of effective performance and proceeded along its byways step by step. You are being transformed into a performance consultant. In the next chapter, you'll discover more about what this means.

Chapter 6

From Training Order-Taker to Performance Consultant

Chapter Highlights:

◆ Your new mission
◆ Your key roles as a performance consultant

The title of the book, *Training Ain't Performance*, is more than a cutsie title. We sincerely consider it as a wake-up call to everyone who views "training" as the winning solution to performance success. We aren't knocking the devotion to wanting to help people learn so that they can perform better. It's a noble and valued cause. We, ourselves, are educators. The point where we diverge from the training path is in the view that training is almost always necessary and frequently sufficient to achieve business results. We are also uncomfortable with what is often a parochialism and insularity within the training community. Time to bust out!

Your New Mission

You work in a state-of-the-art manufacturing facility for a leading-edge biotechnology firm. The pace is fast; the competition fierce. Your work involves developing training for new hires and building programs when new or revised standard operating procedures and government regulations appear. You also play a strong role in the "soft skills area," developing and organizing training on interpersonal, communications, and supervisory skills. In addition, you work on career development projects. In other words, to a large degree, your life and focus center on identifying training needs (strange term), developing the training or buying it, and ensuring quality delivery. That's the mission.

Meanwhile, down in the plant, major business issues are surfacing. There's a new product rollout, and we have to guarantee delivery now that we have FDA approval. We're having quality control issues. Batches of various products we produce aren't meeting stringent quality standards. We also have sealing issues, inspection issues, packaging problems, and distribution headaches. This isn't even the complete list.

So there you are . . . and there they are. Based on this scenario, your focus is on (check one):

- ☐ **Getting the training up and ready and making sure it's delivered on time and with quality.**
- ☐ **The performance problems of the plant.**

The plant manager and her team are focused on (check one):

- ☐ **Getting the training up and ready and making sure it's delivered on time and with quality.**
- ☐ **The performance problems of the plant.**

If you are truly honest, you checked off the training concern for yourself and the performance one for the plant folks. We aren't faulting anyone for this discrepancy. We are using this to make a major point.

 We have to align ourselves very closely with our client's business issues and their performance needs. Our mission is, in partnership with our clients, to produce accomplishments, through people, that all stakeholders value. This includes the people-performers themselves, managers, the organization as a whole, customers, regulatory agencies, and even stretching outward to the community at large.

Think about our biotech firm; safe, effective drugs to ensure health, produced efficiently and profitably, and made available in a timely, effective manner serves everyone's best interests.

Your New Roles

When you are focused on training, your roles generally involve curriculum design, training design, training delivery, training administration (scheduling, enrollment, tracking), and evaluation of learning. As you transform from training order-taker to performance consultant, you confront a new set of roles. Some require a minimal shift in the way you currently act. Others require you to stretch very far. That's OK.

What are these new roles? The essential ones are consultant, analyst, selector-designer-developer-implementer, project manager, facilitator, and monitor. Examine each role in turn. After each one, check off if you feel confident that you can do it, need some help to become proficient, or are really ill at ease with the role and require serious development.

CONSULTANT

Your consulting role encompasses two sets of responsibilities. One involves the whole range of activities to build a partnership relationship with your client organizations. This includes building personal and professional credibility that has them believing you can truly help them solve their problems. The role requires you to listen, provide wise counsel and process expertise, and generally pave the way for project success. This is a highly collaborative role.

The main weapon you possess is your ability to influence your organizational partners to analyze, think, and make decisions systematically and support them when the going gets tough.

You become the person most familiar with the performance improvement requirements; provide information and guidance to all who are involved in the project; review analysis and development work; and recommend next steps, changes, or directions to take. Your key role as a consultant is to act as a project mentor and memory.

Consultant responsibilities include:

- Supervising the analysis steps
- Guiding and managing the client in the initial steps
- Assisting development teams with activities
- Organizing and arranging progress and decision-making meetings
- Communicating project vision
- Identifying resources
- Providing guidance and counsel as required
- Reviewing draft ideas and materials
- Interpreting client needs to designers and developers and vice-versa.

Based on the role description and responsibilities, check off your perception of your capability.

- ☐ **I can do this.**
- ☐ **I can do some of this, but I'll need help to become proficient.**
- ☐ **This is over my head. I need serious development.**

ANALYST

Often you play the role of analyst and consultant simultaneously. Specifically, the analyst role requires that you probe to identify the true business need, determine desired and current performance states, define the performance gap and the relevant factors, and identify suitable interventions. You report these in a data-driven manner to the client.

Analyst responsibilities include:

- Defining business needs
- Defining desired human performance in specific terms
- Characterizing (through analysis) the gap and the gap factors, and identifying the most cost-effective and efficient performance improvement interventions
- Developing suitable information gathering tools
- Writing analysis reports that communicate clearly to stakeholders.

Based on the role description and responsibilities, check off your perception of your capability.

- ☐ **I can do this.**
- ☐ **I can do some of this, but I'll need help to become proficient.**
- ☐ **This is over my head. I need serious development.**

SELECTOR-DESIGNER-DEVELOPER-IMPLEMENTER

In this role, you select, create, and help implement the interventions. You have the client's confidence and authority to carry out all of these tasks. On small-scale projects, you may do all or most of this yourself. In larger ones, you work with internal and perhaps external resources. This is a heavy "doer" role.

Selector-designer-developer responsibilities include:

- Selecting interventions along with rationales for each selection
- Establishing time and action calendars for design, development, and implementation
- Designing/developing interventions
- Partnering with clients to implement interventions
- Acting as a main "general contractor" resource, drawing from support services, technical specialists, and outside vendors as appropriate
- Managing the complete project.

Based on the role description and responsibilities, check off your perception of your capability.

☐ **I can do this.**
☐ **I can do some of this, but I'll need help to become proficient.**
☐ **This is over my head. I need serious development.**

PROJECT MANAGER

In this role, you assume primary responsibility for every phase. You not only partner with your client, you also represent him or her. You are charged with gathering resources; managing all project activities; verifying and monitoring progress; and, in general, acting as the client's agent.

Project manager responsibilities include:

- Setting target dates and managing timelines and responsibilities
- Managing budgets for the project
- Establishing resource selection criteria
- Identifying and selecting resources
- Managing all aspects of the project
- Obtaining client approvals and support
- Mediating
- Facilitating
- Consulting
- Verifying and approving
- Negotiating changes in scope with development teams and clients to adjust timelines and budgets
- Ensuring successful implementation.

Based on the role description and responsibilities, check off your perception of your capability.

☐ **I can do this.**
☐ **I can do some of this, but I'll need help to become proficient.**
☐ **This is over my head. I need serious development.**

FACILITATOR

In this role, you are available to make things easier. This assumes that the client or his or her agent is running the show. Yours is a backseat role, stepping in when requested to help the project proceed smoothly.

Facilitator responsibilities include:

- Finding resources on request
- Explaining to client or development/implementation team members their tasks when requirements of each are not clear

- Facilitating meetings
- Mediating
- Monitoring and assisting as appropriate.

Based on the role description and responsibilities, check off your perception of your capability.

☐ **I can do this.**
☐ **I can do some of this, but I'll need help to become proficient.**
☐ **This is over my head. I need serious development.**

MONITOR

In this role, you still have some project accountability even though the client or others are now doing all of the work. You act as an interested account manager, verifying activities and maintaining contact with client and work teams to ensure all is going as planned.

Monitor responsibilities include:

- Periodically contacting the client to verify degree of satisfaction
- Periodically contacting work teams to verify progress and quality of output
- Providing information, support, and expertise as appropriate
- Keeping the performance consulting group within the organization informed of project status.

Based on the role description and responsibilities, check off your perception of your capability.

☐ **I can do this.**
☐ **I can do some of this, but I'll need help to become proficient.**
☐ **This is over my head. I need serious development.**

Pulling It All Together

As you can see, there are a variety of roles and responsibilities bound up in performance consulting, the main purpose of which is to bring about valued performance from people—performance valued by all stakeholders. What you probably discovered is that you can do a lot of it already. The resources at the back of this book can help a great deal as well. Most of all what you need is experience and seasoning. Joining a local chapter or the international body of the International Society for Performance Improvement (ISPI) or the American Society for Training & Development (ASTD) will also help move you along on a new and fascinating career path. Both of these organizations offer a certification program, Certified Performance Technologist. Check this out at www.astd.org or at www.ispi.org.

Basically, as Dana and Jim Robinson point out in their book, *Performance Consulting: Moving Beyond Training* (1995), you require four essential areas of knowledge and skill to be successful:

- ◆ Business knowledge
- ◆ Knowledge of human performance improvement
- ◆ Partnering skill
- ◆ Consulting skill.

For business knowledge, learn what drives the business. Practice talking "business," not "training." Align yourself with valued business accomplishments and metrics.

For knowledge about human performance improvement, you've already taken a big step by interacting with this book. Explore the recommended resources. Join the professional societies.

Partnering skills come from commitment to working with clients to achieve their valued results. Playing all the roles mentioned above, getting feedback from your clients, and sharing in project responsibilities will soon hone your partnering skills. Collaboration is key.

As for consulting, you are probably doing a lot of this already. Do more. Move from the order-taker stance to one of offering more than just training. By applying the EEP Model, you automatically step into the consultant role.

To end this chapter, how about participating in a series of performance consulting scenarios? We'll provide a variety of these that include your decision to play a particular role in helping the client. The roles are listed and numbered in the right-hand column. Match up the role name with your decision in each scenario. A role name may be used more than once.

Performance consulting services	Performance consulting roles
☐ **A.** The production manager is upset because his work teams appear to be unproductive and also seem to bicker a lot. He asks you for team-building training. You want to first figure out what's going on.	1. Consultant 2. Analyst 3. Selector-designer-developer-implementer 4. Project manager 5. Facilitator 6. Monitor

(continued on page 88)

Performance consulting services	Performance consulting roles
☐ **B.** Gina is a new CFO. She is shocked at how managers throughout the company seem to be incapable of managing their budgets. Errors keep growing, threatening to overwhelm Finance and Accounting's resources. She has heard about your achievements and comes to you for help. She is very open to suggestion. You decide to work hand-in-hand with her.	1. Consultant 2. Analyst 3. Selector-designer-developer-implementer 4. Project manager 5. Facilitator 6. Monitor
☐ **C.** You spotted opportunities for the distribution group to improve on-time deliveries and laid out a plan for Giorgio, the director of distribution, to follow for improving performance. He's keen to move ahead and has organized a task force to develop and implement your recommendations. You will keep in contact with Giorgio and his team, helping out as appropriate.	1. Consultant 2. Analyst 3. Selector-designer-developer-implementer 4. Project manager 5. Facilitator 6. Monitor
☐ **D.** As a one-person learning and performance support department for Fit n' Trim's 20 healthy fast-food stores, you've spotted a lot of variability in drive-through revenues, even though all locations are very similar geographically and demographically. You've analyzed the situation and identified a series of interventions that will probably greatly increase drive-through productivity. You have the general manager's approval to go for it, but no additional budget. You're going to do it anyway!	1. Consultant 2. Analyst 3. Selector-designer-developer-implementer 4. Project manager 5. Facilitator 6. Monitor
☐ **E.** "I love what you've come up with!" enthuses Daniella, the marketing director. "I want it all. Tell me what the budget is. I'll approve. You make it happen." And so you will.	1. Consultant 2. Analyst 3. Selector-designer-developer-implementer 4. Project manager 5. Facilitator 6. Monitor
☐ **F.** After the analysis and recommendations, Ahmed, the head of design teams, took over. Initially things went well. But now other projects are creating competition for people's time and resources. Nevertheless, management wants Ahmed's performance improvement project to succeed. You promised Ahmed you would help sort things out as required. Now, at his request, you're stepping in and calling a meeting.	1. Consultant 2. Analyst 3. Selector-designer-developer-implementer 4. Project manager 5. Facilitator 6. Monitor

Ready for feedback?

A – 2 You want to find out more. This is an analyst role.

B – 1 She hasn't come with a solution. She wants a consultant who will help her achieve success.

C – 6 Giorgio and his team have taken over. You will monitor.

D – 3 You love the challenge and will do it all: select, design, develop, and help implement.

E – 4 You'll make it happen as project manager.

F – 5 Someone needs to help set priorities with key players, and negotiate time and resources—in other words, a facilitator.

Remember This

You've just completed another chapter. Well done. More interesting learning and challenges await you up ahead. To access them, you have to first cross over the review bridge. Please select what you consider to be the better or best option for each of the following statements.

1. Training as a single solution is almost (always/never) sufficient to achieve desired workplace performance.
2. The focus of the training professional is (to get the training up and ready and make sure it's delivered on time and with quality/the performance problems of the workplace).
3. The focus of the performance consultant is (to get the training up and ready and make sure it's delivered on time and with quality/the performance problems of the workplace).
4. The business issues and performance needs of our clients are (the same as/different from) those of the performance consultant.
5. Our mission is to produce, through people, accomplishments that (our clients/all stakeholders) value.
6. In your consulting role, you go about your work (independently of/in partnership with) your clients.
7. Your main strategy, as a performance consultant, is to (do the work of/influence) your clients.
8. In the project manager role, (you assume/your client assumes) primary responsibility for the activities and outcomes of each phase of a project.
9. An essential knowledge area for the performance consultant is (business knowledge/knowledge management).
10. Professional societies such as ASTD and ISPI provide (business knowledge/knowledge of human performance improvement).

Examine and reflect upon the answers.

1. Training as a single solution is almost never sufficient to achieve workplace performance. Training can build knowledge and skills, but, as you've seen, it takes a lot more than any one single intervention to produce workplace performance success.

2. The focus of the training professional is to get the training up and ready and make sure it's delivered on time and with quality. As the title suggests, training is the focus. Making sure the training produces desired learning is a valid concern for training professionals.

3. The focus of the performance consultant is the performance problems of the workplace. The performance consultant is cause-conscious, not solution-focused. What's the performance gap and why is there one? These are appropriate concerns for the performance consultant.

4. The business issues and performance needs of our clients are the same as those of the performance consultant. Now we're talking alignment between client and consultant focus.

5. Our mission is to produce, through people, accomplishments that all stakeholders value. Certainly we want to satisfy our clients. However, to truly succeed, all stakeholders including clients, targeted performers, customers, management, shareholders, even the community at large should share in the performance success.

6. In a consulting role, you go about your work in partnership with your clients. This is an essential part of the performance consulting mission—shared responsibility, shared rewards.

7. Your main strategy, as a performance consultant, is to influence your clients. Influence is the major weapon in your consulting arsenal. You work in partnership. You take on tasks for the client, especially in a project management role. You may often do work away from the client. However, you always maintain the partnership.

8. In the project manager role, you assume primary responsibility for the activities and outcomes of each phase of a project. This is an essential part of the project manager's job. However, ultimate responsibility for meeting business objectives always resides with the client.

9. An essential knowledge area for the performance consultant is business knowledge. Know the business. Use the language of business. Keep your eye on business issues and goals. But also maintain your unique performance consulting

perspective. With respect to knowledge management, it is helpful to learn about it. However, this is not—fascinating as it may be—a fundamental knowledge area for the performance consultant.

10. Professional societies such as ASTD and ISPI provide knowledge of human performance improvement. Business knowledge for performance consultants is largely gained through experience in the workplace.

We have been hammering away at the theme that training ain't performance since the first page. You have encountered a lot of arguments to support this premise along the way. In the next chapter, we delve into this assertion more systematically. Turn the page to discover why training frequently fails.

Chapter 7

Why Training Fails: Maybe Necessary . . . Rarely Sufficient

Chapter Highlights:

◆ Shortcut method to identifying when training isn't the answer
◆ Why transfer of training doesn't just happen

"I need a training program on . . ." is the opening gambit in what often precedes a tale of performance inadequacy. You've heard it so often that you immediately anticipate not only the request for training to be handed to you but also the expectation that you will provide performance problem relief. What you're in fact hearing is, "I've got a problem. You fix it . . . with training." You've already learned the perfect response: "I can help you solve your problem." You have also acquired a model and tools to help your distressed client without promising or delivering unnecessary training. Now, it's time for you to learn a shortcut method to rapidly spotting those cases that are very unlikely to require major training efforts and investments.

This chapter begins with a cast of suspicious characters whose appearance will immediately tip you off to be on your guard against unnecessary training. It then examines the issue of transfer of training to the job and why it usually doesn't happen. It concludes with training that was necessary, yet, somehow, just didn't work.

Suspicious Sayings to Twitch Your Antennae

Check off the sentences or phrases in the list below that you have heard in the past as they accompany a request for training.

- [ ] **My employees are practicing and trying out what they're supposed to know right in front of customers. Fix the training!**

- [ ] **They just didn't get it the last time they were trained. They need retraining.**

- [ ] **They went through all that training but they still don't seem to be able to do it. They need more or better training.**

- [ ] **I don't understand. They passed the certification tests and still can't get the jobs done. You had better give them advanced training.**

- [ ] **We trained them on how to do the job. But, boy, are they slow! We need to train them on how to do it fast.**

- [ ] **We keep increasing our training time without getting better results. What other training should we include?**

- [ ] **We select them carefully for the job. Then we invest in the training. But the washout rate on the job remains high. Could you come up with a new training approach?**

- [ ] **Our training seems to be great. They learn well and can do the job fine. Then they leave us. Maybe we should change the way we train them. Our training is getting to have too good a reputation in the industry.**

Are your antennae twitching? They should be because each of these cases strongly suggests that whatever you or anyone else does, training probably won't be the answer. Let's see why.

- ◆ *My employees are practicing and trying out what they're supposed to know right in front of customers. Fix the training!* It may be that the training didn't provide enough practice or wasn't sufficiently hands-on. However, if employees are practicing in front of customers, you should suspect that they are receiving insufficient coaching and feedback on the job. Too frequently, trainees are trained and then sent out to face customers without some form of transitional scaffolding.

    Prescription: Review the current training, but examine the support structure and feedback mechanisms to strengthen them. Clarify work standards and expectations.

- ◆ *They just didn't get it the last time they were trained. They need retraining.* "Retraining" and "refresher training" are two highly suspect terms. Perhaps training was poor. More than likely, other culprits require investigation.

Prescription: Check to see if the original gap that triggered the training intervention was based on a skill and knowledge deficit. If they didn't get it the first time, something is suspicious. Redo the analysis.

◆ *They went through all that training, but they still don't seem to be able to do it. They need more or better training.* Perhaps. Better to verify first if selection is an issue. Do they have the prerequisites? How are they being supported post-training? Are there disincentives for doing it right?

Prescription: Before going to more or better training, verify selection criteria on characteristics as well as prerequisite skills and knowledge. Check the resources, standards, and support system. Identify competing priorities or task interferences that inhibit essential performances. Read the following case as an example.

Case: Clean Up Your Act!

The new motto for Big Bob's car dealership is: *Customer Service. That's our only job!* To this end, Big Bob has brought in a customer service training program and invested heavily in having everyone go through it. He personally has participated in every session to show support.

In the Parts Department, Jose and Jessica have taken their training to heart. Right over their counter is the new motto in bright red on gold, the dealership colors. The customer flow has been steady and continuous all morning long. They have been serving customers fast, taking time to pull out parts for comparison and to offer alternatives. That is, until the manager, Jeb, spotting all these parts lying around, shouted out of his office, "Hey! What are all those parts doing out there? Get them back in their bins, pronto! We can't have messy counters here."

Five minutes later Big Bob, wandering through Parts, encounters impatient customers waiting at the counter while Jose and Jessica appear to be in the back binning parts. He stomps out furious that the training didn't work.

◆ *I don't understand. They passed the certification tests and still can't get the job done. You had better give them advanced training.* Whoa! Certified and still can't do it? Advanced training will have a low probability of success if the basic program didn't work.

Prescription: Start by verifying the certification standards and exams. Often, they require "talk about" knowledge rather than "do" capability. If the certification testing emphasizes memorization and explanation, that's what performers will focus on. Align certification standards and testing to job requirements. Set up labs (virtual or live) for people to practice. Peer-assisted learning or on-the-job mentoring also works well. Snoop for the cause before heading to the fix.

♦ *We trained them on how to do the job. But, boy, are they slow! We need to train them on how to do it fast.* Training builds basic skills and knowledge. Speed, or fluency, comes only with practice and feedback.

Prescription: Set ever-more-demanding standards for performers to attain—but these must be attainable with practice. Create opportunities for timed practice exercises. Reward increasing success. Provide corrective feedback on process if there is a problem. Recheck work processes. At this point, no more training.

♦ *We keep increasing our training time without getting better results. What other training should we include?* There is considerable research demonstrating the value of parceling out smaller portions of training with time in between allocated for on-job practice. It takes time to assimilate new knowledge and apply it well.

Prescription: Don't include anything more in the training. Reduce it wherever possible and break it up. Focus on on-job practice (e.g., practical experiences, team participation, internships) with graduated challenges and feedback. Provide job aids. Analyze the current training to see what you can eliminate or postpone for later skill upgrading.

♦ *We select them carefully for the job. Then we invest in the training. But the washout rate on the job remains high. Could you come up with a new training approach?* Sure. "We can help you solve your problem." Not necessarily with training, however. Questions to raise include: "Are the selection criteria focused only on competencies and not on characteristics?" "Are job expectations clearly defined as well as standards?" "Are they receiving necessary guidance and support, especially in the initial period post-training?"

Prescription: Begin by finding the answers to the above questions. Good, well-trained people don't usually wash out unless there are obstacles or job nuances that affect their confidence or hidden "killers" in the environment. Read the case on page 97 as an illustration of this.

Surprisingly, we forget that even very bright, capable people can feel lost and insecure in new job environments. There's far more to building performance than a week's training.

Prescription: Verify how these high performers are transitioned from training to the workplace. Establish graduated expectations with management. Ensure frequent and continuous feedback. Initially, pair the performer with an experienced, compatible peer. Create a communication flow between

---

Case: Top Gun Gone

"To become a corporate buyer, you have to have a triple E engineering degree, an MBA in Procurement, and at least 10 years of experience. You are a strategic player, highly paid, and in charge of spending hundreds of millions of dollars."

Maria remembered all of this and was proud and excited when she was selected three months ago from a tough field of candidates. The company had spent a fortune to hire her. So why wasn't it working now? As soon as she was hired and went through a week of training, she was turned loose to do her job.

"I should know what to do, but I still feel awkward. Everyone around here seems so competent. My boss is always busy so I can't bug her. Anyway, I'm supposed to be good. Maybe I'm not. Maybe this isn't the job for me. Look, last week Andy left, and he's really smart. He was great at his old job. My predecessor only lasted six months. I guess you have to be really exceptional in this place. I think that I don't fit in here. I'd better start looking elsewhere."

---

performers and managers. Remember: High performance capability does not always mean high self-confidence in new situations.

♦ *Our training seems to be great. They learn well and can do the job fine. Then they leave us. Maybe we should change the way we train them. Our training is getting to have too good a reputation in the industry.* If the training is great, be delighted. Don't decrease the quality. This is a strong indicator that the training is fine, but other factors are not. If employees are leaving it may be because of inadequate compensation, rewards, recognition, or feedback. They may feel that they are in a dead-end job. Investigate more thoroughly.

Prescription: Verify why employees are leaving, and where they are going. If the position is entry-level and there is no defined career path, ambitious, capable employees will soon leave. Definitely examine the environmental and emotional/political factors first. Increase the value of what they are doing. This is not a training issue.

What you should take away from this section is that the default "training" intervention is the frequent favorite of many of your clients. Keep a sharp eye and ear out for suspicious-sounding reasons why they are making the training choice. The more attuned you are to these, the more rapidly you'll be able to diagnose the true basis of their difficulty and "solve their problem."

But I've Got a Box to Check

Speaking of diagnosis and prescription, here is a rather pernicious malady you may frequently encounter. It's called "check the box syndrome." The case below characterizes it well.

Case: But It's on the List

Marketing Manager (MM): The new system is just a few weeks away from rollout. Let's talk about the training.

Performance Consultant (PC): Sure, what about it?

MM: Well, we've got to train the salesforce on it, you know. We have 200 sales reps spread over the continent, and I've got to get them trained.

PC: I understand, and I can help you solve your problem. From my study of the documentation and discussions with the engineers, the new system appears to be an advanced version of the current one. Positioning hasn't changed. The salesforce seems to be doing a good job with the present system. My analysis shows that the reps really feel confident they can sell the new system. What they seem to need are a great Website and excellent quick reference materials as well as success cases they can show customers. Sales managers concur with this recommendation. They feel ready to run with the new model and are excited about it.

MM: That's all very well and good. But you don't understand. My checklist includes training. I have to show it's being done. So let's focus on that.

This is quite a common tale. What do you do in this case? Select your choice from the following menu:

- ☐ **Fold and offer training**
- ☐ **Do something else and call it training**
- ☐ **Listen; acknowledge; come back with data and alternative costs, lost opportunity numbers, and options including, if necessary and useful, some form of training (e.g., brief self-study, Webinar, Webcast)**

Obviously the first choice is the easy and line-of-least-resistance choice. However, by now you should be convinced that this is an unproductive, unprofessional route to follow. You probably rejected it. The second choice is tempting. There's a bit of a deceptive element here, although we admit to having strayed toward this choice occasionally as a last resort. The best choice, by far, is the third. Let the data talk. You will still be up against that all-important box to be checked off, but if you are forced to provide training, you will have given your client much food for thought when the next encounter occurs.

Job Security for Trainers: A Vested Interest in Performance Failure

We once worked with an automotive company that was experiencing well over 100 percent annual turnover in its dealership salesforces. The corporate training group created and sold sales training to the dealers. Innocently, we asked our client why they weren't more focused on solving the horrendous turnover problem. With a smile and a wink, he whispered to us, "And lose this gold mine of customers for our courses?"

Fortunately, not all training groups or professionals think this way. However, many do voice concerns about how to charge for nontraining services and interventions. This is justifiable. Training is easy to cost out and bill for. How do you charge for several days of analysis and a one-page job aid that saves many thousands of dollars?

The answer is: "Not easy." Value is what you and your clients are really after. You will have to establish a pricing or cost model that is equitable to all. Some organizations fund a central learning and performance support group and then have clients draw services from it on a fair share basis. Others establish key performance indicators for the learning and performance support group and use a Customer Review Board to assess value quarterly. Still others operate very similarly to outside vendors, using account managers who write proposals and bill for services in a variety of ways.

Whatever the formula, what is certain is that most leading-edge organizations are transforming their training groups into some form of performance consulting/ services entity. Job security is shifting away from training order-taking to systemic performance support.

Training Was the Answer, but It Just Didn't Stick

Your analysis concluded that a key factor affecting the performance gap was lack of skills and knowledge. You recommended training, which was highly interactive, content relevant, and included lots of practice. Yet, when you checked to see how well your trainees were performing back on the job, you were disappointed to discover that they were still doing things the old way. There was little sign of transfer to the job. Have you ever experienced this frustrating situation? Select your response.

☐ **Yes**
☐ **No**

No? Then you are a rare individual. Research on transfer to the workplace strongly suggests that much of training evaporates into thin air shortly after the training events have occurred. Three months later, evidence suggests that in most cases only 10 to 30 percent remains. What a loss! Fortunately, you have not experienced this.

Yes? Welcome to the majority group. We hope you are frustrated by this state of affairs and eager to do something about it.

Chapter 7

The Story of Transfer

By transfer, we are referring to the use of what was acquired in training back on the job. One would think that this would occur naturally. After all, why train if they aren't going to use it? (A question we have frequently asked ourselves.) So, let's see what really does happen.

Case: Hit Those Keys

Ivan was fed up with his inability to type faster. His hunt-and-peck method, which he had developed on his own, allowed him to trundle along at about 25 words a minute with occasional errors. He had resigned himself to this state until, in a meeting, he discovered that most of his peers could touch-type at a rate of 70 to 100 words per minute with very few errors. "Enough!" he decided. "I'm taking a keyboard course."

The course lasted two days and was fast-paced with lots of practice. Ivan had a great deal of difficulty getting the feel of things, especially with covered keys. However, he persisted and by the end of the course could do the final test at 35 words a minute without looking at the keys. He still made errors.

Back on the job, Ivan was resolved to use his newly acquired skills. Then came the crunch.

"Hey, Ivan," his boss called to him. "You've been gone a couple of days. I desperately need your report by noon. I'm presenting it to the management team. Have it ready."

Ivan immediately flung himself into action. He had three and a half hours to deadline. He immediately hit the keys, trying to practice what he had just learned. Alas. Trying to compose the report and remember all the keys and finger placements were simply too much for him. There was also the pressure.

Ivan soon found himself confused and going slower than before the course, with increased errors. In a panic, Ivan finally abandoned his newly acquired skill set and settled back into his old familiar hunt-and-peck style. Ah! Much better. He would make the deadline.

What happened to Ivan occurs regularly in the workplace. The conditions and pressures of the environment remain the same, even though, through training, the person has changed. Without support and encouragement, the inertia of the system plus the familiarity of old habits soon smother even the best training. Here is how it works. Examine Figure 7-1. It's divided into three phases: before, during, and after training. Imagine that Ivan's typing state is initially at 25 words per minute and the ideal is 80 words per minute. This is his starting state.

Ivan then enters training. During training, there is an initial period of adjustment, but with instruction, support, practice, and feedback, Ivan begins to progress as in Figure 7-2.

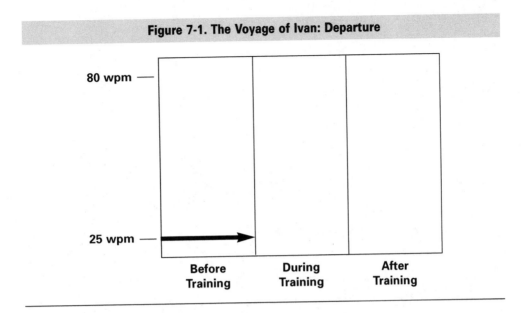

Figure 7-1. The Voyage of Ivan: Departure

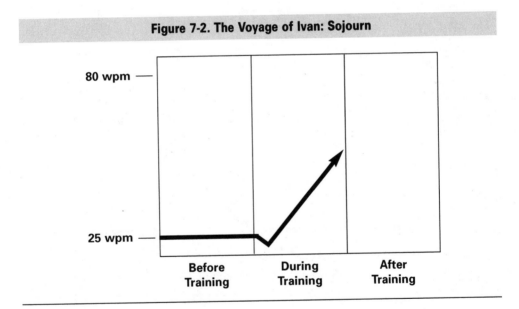

Figure 7-2. The Voyage of Ivan: Sojourn

You would then expect that once Ivan leaves training and returns to his workplace, progress should continue as in Figure 7-3.

Sadly, reality proves otherwise. The same conditions as existed before, old habits, and lack of support generally result in what is shown in Figure 7-4, which occurred in Ivan's case.

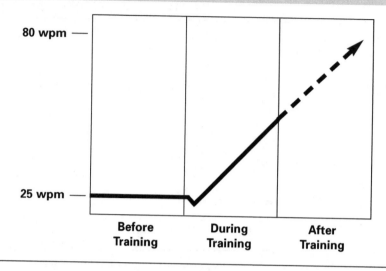

Figure 7-3. The Voyage of Ivan: Return Expectations

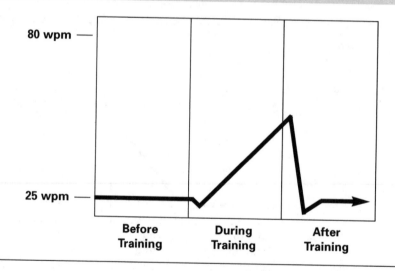

Figure 7-4. The Voyage of Ivan: Return Reality

Can anything be done about this? Yes. Imagine the same three states of before, during, and after. Also, think of the three key players in the transfer context: the trainee, the trainer, and the supervisor. Mary Broad and John Newstrom, in their book *Transfer of Training* (1992), demonstrated how each player, at each stage, can contribute to the promotion of transfer. Examine Worksheet 7-1, which shows the stages and players. Select the three most important cells for promoting transfer. They are labeled A, B, C, D, and so forth.

Worksheet 7-1. Stages and Players of Transfer

Players	Period before training	Period during training	Period after training
Supervisor	A	B	C
Trainee	D	E	F
Trainer	G	H	I

Write in your cell selections here.

What Mary Broad and John Newstrom found from their research—and we heartily agree—is that A, G, and C are the most important for encouraging transfer. Thinking this through in performance consulting terms makes these selections logical choices.

- **A**—What the supervisor does before the trainee goes to training has an enormous impact on how the trainee thinks and acts during and after. Imagine that Ivan's boss had said, "Ivan, you're going to a typing class next week. That's great. Let's talk about how this will help you in your work. What will we have to do to support you on your return?" That sends a positive message, doesn't it?

- **G**—What the trainer—or here we can substitute performance consultant or performance consultant and trainer together—does prior to the training event can make a world of difference. Check off in the list below those items you believe have the potential to significantly increase the probability of transfer. We'll meet you at the end of this exercise.

  - ☐ **Create materials and job aids to help supervisors prepare employees for training.**
  - ☐ **Design the training to focus on high-priority job tasks.**
  - ☐ **Design a lot of practice exercises that lead directly to real-world tasks.**
  - ☐ **Include strong rationales based on job-related results for encouraging trainees to engage actively in the training and supervisors to support it.**
  - ☐ **Create materials and job aids to be used in the training that can then be reused back on the job.**
  - ☐ **Create materials and job aids to help supervisors debrief training and support on-job application of learning.**
  - ☐ **Help establish technical and other forms of support mechanisms to assist in the transfer of learning and on-job application.**

  You probably checked off all of the items. So did we.

♦ **C**—What the supervisor does as soon as Ivan returns to the job from training also has a strong effect on transfer. Again, imagine the boss saying, "Ivan, now that you're back from training, I'd like you to put what you've learned to work on the report for today's meeting. If you need help with parts of the report, I'll get Jo to help you. It's important that you practice typing the right way or you'll soon fall back to your old method and the training will have been wasted."

This may sound fanciful and yet it requires such little effort. The result is increased motivation to apply the new learning and encouragement to persist.

You could go through each of the cells in Worksheet 7-1 and imagine ways to encourage transfer of training to the job. We will leave this exercise and reflection to you as we summarize our key points.

 Training is one of the ways to achieve desired performance. It is a relevant consideration when there's a skill and knowledge deficiency. It will not achieve results, however, if left to itself. Training still ain't performance without careful consideration of how to support transfer back on the job.

Training Was the Answer and They Supported It. Still . . .

We close this chapter on why training fails with a final section that presents a few additional factors that influence the impact of training. In one sense, they are beyond the scope of the performance consultant to alter radically. Nevertheless, once aware of these factors, you can help decrease their impact by educating management through the data you gather in your analysis investigations. Rather than describe these to you, we invite you to find them yourself. Study each mini-case on page 105 and match it with the most probable reason the training didn't achieve the targeted outcomes. Place the number of the reason in the box beside the case. There are more reasons than cases. You may use the same reason more than once. When you have finished, let's compare selections.

Our selections, in order, are: 4, 5, 1, 2, and 3. They all underscore the same theme. Even when training is necessary, it can seldom do the job alone. This is another reason why training professionals must transform themselves into a larger performance role.

 Remember This

This chapter focused on why training fails, not why training is a failure. Its central message to you is, "Think systemically." No single intervention can achieve performance success in isolation from others. To reinforce key

Mini-Case	Reason
☐ The training on customer service was innovative, participatory, and job relevant. Supervisors and managers were prepared to support the new customer service campaign. Yet not much changed. Front-line workers firmly believed that processing customer orders was the bottom line and that's how they would be judged. "That's all management cares about. Customer service, what's in it for me?"	1. Lack of career path. 2. Faulty process. 3. Threatening atmosphere/culture. 4. Lack of perceived value. 5. Perceived unfairness or lack of equity. 6. Lack of funds.
☐ The training resulted in everyone being able to demonstrate how to transform a service call to a sales call. Management was there to help make it happen. "But only outbound sales reps get the big commissions," complained the service reps. "And that's not right!"	
☐ Despite the excellent training and support, we lose a lot of our agents before a year is out. The pay is competitive. The working conditions are very good. Still, they leave because they see no future for themselves.	
☐ We trained the payroll clerks on the new system and have lots of technical support if they run into trouble. They seem to bog down in having to search our three databases for the required data, then enter the data, and finally verify accuracy. There are 11 steps to follow and the Information Technology Department assures us that they are all logical.	
☐ The training is thorough. We have inspectors who watch workers at each step in the process. As soon as they spot an error, they step in, note it, and correct the worker. But as soon as the inspectors are no longer watching, errors occur. The workers seem not to be able to function without constant supervision.	

points, here's a final review. Please select the appropriate alternative in each of the following statements and then examine the feedback.

1. Training is often (necessary/sufficient), but rarely (necessary/sufficient) to produce long-term performance.

2. If they are not performing as desired after they were trained, (provide refresher training/suspect that this is not a skill and knowledge issue).

3. If they can't perform after doing well on the certification test, suspect the (training/test).

4. Bright, capable people who have demonstrated past performance success are (generally secure/often insecure) in a new job.

5. Excellent training, well designed and delivered, that produces strong learning results (guarantees/does not guarantee) high rates of transfer to the job.

6. Following effective training, you can expect (continued performance improvement/a performance decrease) if unsupported back on the job.

7. What supervisors do with the trainees before training has a (high/moderate/low) impact on post-training transfer.

8. The training worked well. Managers and supervisors supported and encouraged trainees back on the job. Still, performance didn't change. Suspect (the training/environmental factors).

Here is feedback on your choices.

1. Training is often necessary, but rarely sufficient to produce long-term performance. Very frequently, there are skill and knowledge elements to be acquired. When this is the case, training is a viable option. But not alone.

2. If they are not performing as desired after they were trained, suspect that this is not a skill and knowledge issue. Unless the training was wretched, there are probably other factors of an environmental or emotional-political nature causing the problem.

3. If they can't perform after doing well on the certification test, suspect the test. They did well on the test, so the training was fine. Because the test should reflect real-world requirements, reexamine the test.

4. Bright, capable people who have demonstrated past performance success are often insecure in a new job. In fact, the more ambitious and successful a person is, the more insecure and vulnerable he or she may be in new, challenging settings. Psychologists studying the "imposter syndrome" found that most highly successful people attributed their successes to factors other than their capabilities. This makes them very vulnerable.

5. Excellent training, well designed and delivered, that produces strong learning results does not guarantee high rates of transfer to the job. The trainees must be encouraged and supported to commit, engage, and persist at transfer. The environment must also be attuned to transfer requirements.

6. Following effective training, you can expect a performance decrease if unsupported back on the job. Pretty self-evident by now. Review Figures 7-1 to 7-4 to reinforce this.

7. What supervisors do with the trainees before training has a high impact on post-training transfer. Although this seems chronologically counterintuitive, it does make a big difference. A well prepared and well briefed trainee approaches training differently, participates with more engagement, and is generally more motivated to apply learning to the job.

8. The training worked well. Managers and supervisors supported and encouraged trainees back on the job. Still, performance didn't change. Suspect environmental factors. As we have so frequently pointed out, performance is more frequently affected by environmental than individual factors. Investigate the environment before the individual.

To this point, you have learned a great deal about training and performance—what works and what doesn't. You have a solid foundation upon which to build effective interventions. That's the subject of the next chapter. From analyst, consultant, and strategic thinker, we move to the tactical level. Roll up your sleeves. Get ready to intervene.

Chapter 8

Panoply of Performance Interventions

Chapter Highlights:

◆ What's an intervention?
◆ Nine learning and 10 nonlearning interventions

In this chapter, we get down and dirty, so to speak. We focus on performance interventions: the various types, examples, and ways to apply them. By the end of this chapter, you will have gathered 19 major types of interventions into your performance toolkit. Some may be familiar to you. Others may give you pause as you ask yourself, "Can I do this?" Remember, you don't have to be able to do it all by yourself. As we pointed out earlier, performance consulting includes many roles. It also usually requires teamwork. Use other, specialized resources to create the interventions that are beyond your current capabilities. It's great to involve others. We suspect, however, that you, with the help of resources we have included in the For Further Reading section at the back of this book, will be able to do most of what we present.

What's an Intervention?

Some people hate the word "intervention." It sounds somewhat interfering and coldly clinical. They prefer "solutions" or even "performance enhancements." You choose your term. The common human performance improvement jargon term is *intervention,* so we are sticking with it here.

Simply stated, an intervention is something that is specifically designed to bridge the gap between current and desired performance states. It can be complete unto itself or part of a basket of interventions. It is a deliberately conceived act or system that is strategically applied to produce intended performance results.

Concretely, an intervention is anything the performance consultant—you—can conceive of that is currently absent and the presence of which will result in performance improvement. An intervention can also include removal of an obstacle that prevents performance from occurring.

Quick check. Select from the list below those items you perceive as potential performance interventions.

- ☐ **Redesign of the work environment**
- ☐ **Analysis of a performance gap**
- ☐ **Setting of performance standards**
- ☐ **Removal of time-wasting approvals**
- ☐ **Simplification of reporting forms**
- ☐ **Elimination of interfering tasks**

Feedback time.

- ◆ *Redesign of the work environment.* If there are obstacles in the environment that create barriers to performance and you remove these, or if you change the environmental configuration to improve workflow, collaboration, or even isolation when needed, then you definitely have a performance intervention.
- ◆ *Analysis of a performance gap.* This will lead to recommended interventions, but is not a performance intervention as defined here.
- ◆ *Setting of performance standards.* Definitely a performance intervention that can have a powerful impact. When people know very clearly what the standards are, they can aim toward them. Performance attainment and consistency are the result.
- ◆ *Removal of time-wasting approvals.* Hunting for approval signatures can create horrendous bottlenecks, especially if one of the approvers is on vacation or abroad. Reducing the number of approvals down to the essential ones can speed up performance. It's an intervention.
- ◆ *Simplification of reporting forms.* Another example of an intervention. It may be modest, but if the result is improved or more rapid performance, it counts.

◆ *Elimination of interfering tasks.* This is a wonderful performance intervention. Getting rid of something is generally cheaper than creating something new. More on this later when we examine an entire menu of intervention possibilities along with examples.

You now should have the concept of intervention firmly fixed in your mind. We proceed, then, to two categories of performance interventions. The categorization approach we present is not the only way of organizing interventions. We happen to find it simple, practical, and useful in our performance improvement work. We mention this in case you encounter other ways of clustering interventions elsewhere.

Two Categories of Interventions: Learning and Nonlearning

The two categories we present are learning and nonlearning. We further break down nonlearning interventions into performance aids, environmental interventions, and emotional interventions. These are in line with the way we have clustered performance gap factors: skills and knowledge, environmental, and emotional. The convenience of this approach is that as you identify key factors affecting the gap in your analysis, they usually lead naturally and directly to appropriate interventions. As an example, if your analysis uncovers a lack of resources, part of the environmental grouping of factors affecting the performance gap, the obvious intervention is to provide suitable resources, one of the environmental intervention options. This all sounds too easy. And, for the most part, it is, at least for identifying appropriate interventions. Designing, developing, and implementing these can be another matter.

We now turn to each of the categories and offer you a panoply (impressive array) of performance interventions.

Learning Interventions

Although we have been saying all along that training ain't performance, we have also made it clear that training is a suitable type of intervention to consider when lack of skills and knowledge is a contributing gap factor. Other learning interventions that are not training per se but which achieve performance success are also potentially viable. Let's review what we mean by *learning* and *learning intervention.*

Learning is change. It is an adaptive mechanism that we humans, along with all other animal organisms, are genetically programmed to do. Because each individual organism may encounter different environmental conditions from other members of its species, it must be equipped with adaptive capabilities to meet these unique situations to survive. Learning, therefore, is the ability to change. It is an alteration in our mental structures that results in the potential for behavior change. As an example, if you were to find yourself in a strange land with unknown foods and delectable looking poisonous plants, you would have to "learn" what is edible and what is life threatening. As the possible ingestible items become more familiar, you would build new mental (cognitive) structures that would have an impact on your food selection behaviors.

In the performance arena, learning interventions are the range of actions or events you initiate to help people acquire new skills and knowledge so that they can survive and prosper in the workplace.

Worksheet 8-1 provides you with a continuum of learning interventions, from the very natural to the highly structured. It is far from complete but does offer an interesting array of options. The worksheet lays these out for you individually, but, of course, you can mix and match them to produce highly effective combinations. As you will note, the worksheet not only names each type of learning intervention, it also describes it and suggests sample applications. The fourth column is left blank for you to come up with a possible application in your setting. Please think about each learning intervention and jot down at least one way you could use it to improve performance somewhere in your environment. A number of these should already be familiar to you. We encourage you to stretch your imagination beyond the ordinary for your workplace setting.

From our own experience, here are examples of how we have used each of these learning interventions to help improve performance.

Natural experience—Persons in support service functions for a railway were assigned to a week of work aboard the trains and in the yards. The result: Accountants, human resource specialists, and administrative personnel, among others, obtained firsthand experience on what the railway is about. This led to more responsive and rapid support of railway operation needs—a definite performance improvement.

Experiential learning—Executives (e.g., marketing, finance, procurement) of a fast-food chain of stores were placed on the firing line for one week. Each day concluded with two debriefings. One was led by actual front-line workers and discussed executives' in-store performance as well as issues experienced. The second, for the executives only and led by a performance consultant facilitator, focused on implications for the company and higher-level decision making in light of work experiences. This resulted in significant work process and people management improvements.

Worksheet 8-1. A Continuum of Learning Interventions

Learning intervention	Description/explanation	Sample applications	Application in my setting
Natural experience	The individual or group is placed in the natural environment and learns through real-life trial-and-error events. You might also label this "life experience."	Internship, practicum, assignment to a new team or task-force, temporary job placement, duty rotation	
Experiential learning	Very similar to natural experience. However, the individual or group also participates in structured debriefing sessions to reflect on the experiences encountered and draw conclusions or plan new courses of action.	Practicum, structured and mentored internship, field placement with coaching, on-the-job practice and work sessions, supervised transitional work settings following training	
On-the-job training (informal)	The individual learner assumes an apprenticeship role while working in an operational setting. Co-workers and supervisors informally provide guidance as needed on how to perform.	Apprenticeship program, job placement with orientation and coaching on request, ordinary job placement with instructions to co-workers to "help out"	
Structured-on-the-job training (planned)	Similar to on-the-job training except that the operational work environment has been systematically organized and prepared for learning. The individual "learner" has a roadmap and learning plans to acquire work-relevant skills and knowledge with the assistance of trained lead workers, sometimes called structured-on-the-job trainers (SOJT). Self-evaluation and SOJT forms are usually built into the program.	Structured-on-the-job program, structured mentoring program for newly hired technical personnel, model learn-and-work environments	

(continued on page 114)

Worksheet 8-1. A Continuum of Learning Interventions (continued)

Learning intervention	Description/explanation	Sample applications	Application in my setting
Simulation	The individual performs as she or he would in real life. However, the setting is an artificial creation designed to resemble the natural environment. Simulations range from very realistic (high fidelity) to symbolic and abstract (low fidelity). In all simulations for learning, regardless of degree of fidelity, the critical elements of the job must be represented along with realistic interactions and outcomes.	Physically realistic simulators, virtual reality environments, psychologically realistic settings, in-basket exercises, war games, virtual labs, assessment centers	
Role play	The individual assumes roles other than his or her own real ones or remains the same person but is thrust into settings that are different from the current one. In these novel situations, the individual acts out feelings, reactions, and responses to various scenarios or events.	Psychodramas; sociodramas; group role play for sales, counseling, or management; practice in handling social interactions of all kinds	
Laboratory training	This is similar to simulation training except that the laboratory does not necessarily re-create the work environment. The individual can practice a broad range of work activities, but not necessarily in normal job sequence. The laboratory offers a practice environment and set of experiences where error can be exploited as a powerful opportunity for learning.	Science experimentation, repair practice, hardware/software adaptation and troubleshooting, welding practice, medical experimentation and practice	

Learning intervention	Description/explanation	Sample applications	Application in my setting
Classroom training (live or virtual)	The individual acquires skills and knowledge through guidance from an instructor in a formal group setting removed from the workplace. With interactive distance learning, Webinars, and Webcasts, the individual may be at the work site, but the session is not usually an integrated part of ongoing work activities.	Seminars, workshops, lectures, demonstrations, Internet-based classes, video and audio conferences, Webinars, Webcasts	
Self-study	The individual acquires skills and knowledge through self-learning, guided by structured materials ranging from print to highly sophisticated electronic systems.	Highly directive, programmed instruction, computer-based modules, Web-based virtual labs, CD-ROM/DVD learning modules, embedded learning objects, Web explorations	

On-the-job training—Relocation agents help people transferred by their companies or by government agencies with their move to new locations. This includes selling and buying homes, moving furniture, and finding schools and special services. Following training, the novice agents join work teams and learn the ropes on the job with help from more advanced workers. The assistance they receive is obtained informally. The novices wear a special nametag that says on it, "Please lend a hand." After six weeks, the nametag is removed, usually with a fun, team ceremony. This informal method leads to continuous performance improvement and team integration.

Structured-on-the-job training (SOJT)—The setting was a brewery distribution center where cases and casks of beer and ales arrive from the plant and are received, stacked, stored, and distributed to customers. The pace is rapid. There are many rules to follow. Orders must be precise. Safety is a major issue. There are a large variety of vehicles circulating. A new worker receives an orientation and a learning roadmap. He or she is assigned to a team and receives training on the job from trained lead workers who teach and evaluate task accomplishment before passing the learner on to master the next task. Supervisors and the training department verify progress as appropriate. The learner is responsible for task mastery and for triggering evaluations. The SOJT program has halved learning time and decreased time-to-satisfactory-performance costs by more than 60 percent.

Simulation—Adjusting the operations of the powerful electrolytic cells that convert alumina to aluminum ingots is a highly technical and sophisticated process. To become skilled, operators spent years learning on the job. By creating highly realistic computer-based simulations, performance was improved while decreasing time-to-satisfactory-performance requirements by 40 percent.

Role play—Through the use of structured role plays, police, medical personnel, and legal professionals gained enormous insight into what it is like to be the victim of rape or battering. The result was far greater sensitivity in handling such victims, fewer complaints, and more victims willing to prosecute.

Laboratory training—Through a virtual lab, advanced systems engineers were able to acquire best practices on all relevant aspects of server clusters. This included voluntary self-certification and, via a Website, a venue for global sharing with colleagues of problems, bizarre experiences, and successes. The result was more rapid best-practice acquisition and increased mutual support.

Classroom training—All of us have many examples of these. One of our most exciting was a one-day workshop on designing games and simulations for learning and performance that we conducted with more than 100 parents of children with intellectual disabilities. It was for parents only (no teachers) at an education conference. The parents created some 50 games during the day. They subsequently edited these, published them, and created a network for continued mutual support. This was a real, live happening with wonderful performance outcomes.

Self-study—We once created a self-study multimedia package (video, print, audio-tape, interactive telephone testing system) for the national salesforce of a high-technology company. It was on an entirely new array of products for a new market sector. The package was fun, highly interactive, and contained a great deal of practice, exercises, vocabulary crossword puzzles, sample audio presentations to play in your car, self and peer assessments, and job aids to assist the sales representatives. To cap it off, the sales reps had to dial into an interactive telephone testing system (the Web was not yet ready for this). With major support from senior management, the awarding of prizes, and random spot checks, more than 90 percent of the 600 sales representatives completed the self-study. The result was an immediate and sustained sales spike. Sales goals were surpassed.

Our examples were intended to inspire you. If you did not jot down your own possible applications in Worksheet 8-1 or if you have come up with new ideas since then, please return to the worksheet and record them. We'll wait for you before moving on to nonlearning interventions, the next major category.

Nonlearning Interventions

Nonlearning interventions are actions or events designed to change conditions that facilitate attainment of performance. Anything that removes an obstacle or adds a facilitative element to the performance system qualifies as a nonlearning intervention. Nonlearning interventions fall into three subcategories: performance aids, environmental interventions, and emotional interventions.

PERFORMANCE AIDS

These are external memory aids performers can call on as needed. The two major subcategories of performance aids are job aids and performance support tools and systems. Some are static. They provide information or diagrams carefully displayed so that you can easily find the item that tells you what to do or triggers your action. Others are dynamic and offer a pathway, columns of items to choose from, or actual moving displays (electronically or mechanically) that engage you in activities that lead to a desired outcome or spew out responses. In all cases, job aids and performance support tools and systems contain information and procedures you do not have to learn and remember. They all provide you with the right question, answer, or decision for you at the right moment. *The only learning you have to do is how to use the performance aid.*

Worksheet 8-2 presents you with more information about this great set of performance interventions. It is divided into four columns just like the learning interventions worksheet (8-1). As you read across, imagine a way you might employ one or more types of job aids or performance support tools and jot it down in the fourth column.

Worksheet 8-2. Performance Aid Interventions

Performance aid intervention	Description/explanation	Sample applications	Application in my setting
Job aid	An information repository that helps you perform a task in expert fashion. There are many sorts of job aids from simple to complex: • Step-by-step procedures • Worksheets • Directory displays • Decision trees and tables • Algorithm flowcharts	Beside each type of job aid there are two examples. • Cookbook recipe instructions • Visual steps to assemble a piece of equipment • Form that guides you to calculate your taxes • A template for writing a proposal • List of emergency phone numbers • Glossary of terms with definitions • Table to guide selection of the right employee benefits for you • Tree that guides you to discover the trouble in a piece of equipment • A flowchart that leads you to decide on which valve to open • A flowchart to help decide whether to give a loan	

Performance aid intervention	Description/explanation	Sample applications	Application in my setting
Job aid (continued)	• Checklists • Samples	• Checklist to verify that an order is complete • Checklist that all safety steps have been performed • Displays of different types of layout for different types of newsletters • Manual of ways to cite references for journal articles	
Performance support tools and systems	These performance aids, especially electronic performance support systems (EPSS), are very high-end, sophisticated job aids. They are designed to help you act and make decisions like a high-end expert performer. Some include artificial intelligence programming. More prosaically, performance support systems can help ask the right questions in a call center or troubleshoot a system failure. The key advantages are reduced time, near expert performance almost immediately, and high payback of their costs through time savings and error reduction.	• Conduct a medical diagnosis • Determine whether to launch a missile against an unknown aircraft • Identify the cause of system failure • Book a service call • Fill out a repair order • Run a credit check • Cross-sell products and services • Schedule meetings	

Job aids are usually easy to create and offer almost immediate performance results. They are among our favorite interventions. What we like best about them is that they can be extremely simple, yet powerful. Here is one of our favorites along with its interesting case background.

Case: Transit Tally

"So this is the situation. Most of the riders on our buses and subways use monthly passes that they purchase close to the end of the month or at the beginning of the new month. Most riders buy these at the subway stations. And they usually do this going to and coming from work—at peak hours.

"Our ticket agents sell the monthly passes. Almost all of them—about 400—are former bus drivers who can no longer drive buses due to health problems. Average age is 55. We give them this job so that they can work to retirement and draw full pension. It's an agreement we have with the unions.

"Our big problem is their slow pace and their error rates. We'd like you to train them how to add fast and sell passes accurately. We've never really trained them before. We would automate the sales, but we don't have money to install a new system. We have to fix this problem. Riders are up in arms. The newspapers are hammering us and error rates are out of control. Please get them trained fast."

With this information, Ben reassured his client and then posed a key question. "Are all of the agents slow and inaccurate? Does anyone do it right?"

"For the most part, it's a mess," came the response. "There's only one station where they seem to be getting it right—St. Leo's."

Ben decided to follow up and traveled the subway to St. Leo's station. He arrived just before shift change. After introducing himself, he silently observed the transactions. A rider came up to the window requesting one child's pass, one senior citizen's, and two adult passes.

"That'll be $136 please," the agent immediately responded. Ben did the calculation mentally. One child, $26 and one senior, also $26—both entitled to special passes—and two adults each at $42. It took him about a minute to arrive at the same amount. Amazed at how rapidly the agent had done the calculation, he continued observing more closely. The next transactions also took only a few seconds and were perfectly accurate. That's when Ben noticed a shirt cardboard on the agent's counter with a hand-drawn matrix that looked like this:

Number of regular passes

		0	1	2	3	4	5	6	7	8
Number of special passes	0		42	84	126	168	216	294	294	336
	1	26	66	110	152	194	236	360	360	362
	2	52	94	**136**	178	220	262	346	346	388
	3	78	120	162	204	246	288	372	372	414
	4	104	146	188	**230**	272	314	398	398	440

With this chart, it took only a couple of seconds to determine that passes for two children, two seniors, and three adults came to $230. Fast and error free!

As the agent packed up for the day, he removed his cardboard job aid. The next agent was already waiting to take over. And in her hand, tightly gripped, was a similar shirt cardboard.

Simple. Elegant. Effective. All that was left for Ben to do was make a sturdier, large print and colorful model of the matrix, laminate it, and then circulate to each station demonstrating its use. The result was dramatic. For approximately $500 in materials and a few days of coaching, speed increased by 70 percent overall with a virtual zero error rate. That's performance improvement!

Here is another example of a job aid we really like. It's for training designers who have to create tests to match learning objectives perfectly. The key is to determine whether or not the objective requires procedural ("do") knowledge or declarative ("talk-about") knowledge. The following job aid explains the different types of tests and "verification

---

Exercise: Select the right type/s of tests (can be more than one) for each of the following objectives. Use the job aid below to help you. The tests must match each objective perfectly.

1. Given a list of stain removers, identify which one or ones remove cherry stains from linen.

2. Name the capitals of the European countries with no errors.

3. Given an automobile with a flat tire on a slope, replace the tire with the spare provided.

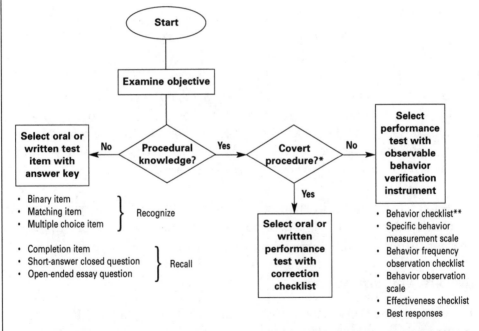

*A covert procedure is one you cannot see being performed. It takes place in the learner's head. Mental arithmetic, troubleshooting, and decision making that occur inside the learner with no overt activity are examples of covert procedures.

**Most common type of performance test.

(continued on page 122)

Type of Test/s	
Objective 1:	
Objective 2:	
Objective 3:	

instruments." Try it out yourself to see if you can select the right type of test for each of the objectives in the following exercise. Remember, examples of procedural knowledge are—ride a bicycle, troubleshoot a piece of equipment, design a circuit. Examples of declarative knowledge are—explain the flow of electricity through a wire, describe the process of digestion, list five criteria for accepting a loan application.

Using the job aid, here is how we responded.

Objective 1: Because this is not procedural knowledge, but talk-about—recognize—knowledge, we selected either a matching test item or a multiple choice test item to measure knowledge of stain removers.

Objective 2: This is also not procedural knowledge, but declarative (talk-about) knowledge of a recall nature. We selected either a completion item or a short answer-closed question test (e.g., "The capitals of the European countries are: _____, _____, _____).

Objective 3: This objective requires the learner to do something. It is procedural knowledge that the learner must demonstrate and it is also not covert (hidden). You can see what is being done as well as verify results. Our selection, therefore, is a performance test accompanied with a behavior/results checklist to verify that the test item meets the criterion for matching "perfectly."

As you can see, this job aid requires more background knowledge than the transit pass matrix. However, it still speeds up and simplifies test selection, which is a rather sophisticated skill. In both cases, the job aids act as external memory devices.

ENVIRONMENTAL INTERVENTIONS

This set of interventions encompasses an extremely broad grouping. It includes all the adjustments you can make within the work environment, either by eliminating barriers that prevent performance or increasing support mechanisms for obtaining and enhancing desired accomplishments. Worksheet 8-3, which lists some environmental interventions, is divided into four columns, the fourth one offering you an opportunity to jot down possible ways you might apply the interventions to your work setting.

Worksheet 8-3. Environmental Interventions

Environmental intervention	Description/explanation	Sample applications	Application in my setting
Provision of information	Lack of clarity of performance expectations and lack of specific, timely feedback focused on how one is performing in light of these expectations combine to form the number one cause of performance deficiencies in the workplace. Other information factors that decrease performance are • Lack of access to required information • Unclear or unavailable policies or procedures • Inaccurate and out-of-date information • Contradictory information • Lack of communication about products, events, and decisions	• Creation of standards for doing the job • Harmonization of conflicting standards • Establishment and communication of unambiguous performance expectations • Provision of current catalogues and lists • Provision of timely and specific information to the individual on how she or he is performing • Development of a company policy on ethical practices • Priority access to databases	
Provision of resources	Without sufficient resources, the individual cannot perform as expected. Too often, workers go through training on a new system and then return to the job where resources to practice and maintain or increase newly acquired skills are lacking.	• Provision of appropriate tools and equipment to perform the job as expected • Provision of sufficient time for task completion • Access to help desks or technical support to encourage performance • Creation of practice environments for newly acquired skills • Increased access to supervisors, specialists, and resource personnel • Development of workable, efficient procedures	

(continued on page 124)

Worksheet 8-3. Environmental Interventions (continued)

Environmental intervention	Description/explanation	Sample applications	Application in my setting
Redesign of the work environment	Inadequate organizational structure, communications systems, work processes, and physical or administrative infrastructures create delays and inhibit performance. Bureaucratic red tape, noisy and uncomfortable surroundings, and poor ventilation all contribute to decreased performance.	• Breakdown of barriers between departments for mutually beneficial decision making and resource sharing • Introduction of communications systems such as instant messaging and file sharing • Redesign of workflow to reduce unnecessary or bottleneck steps • Elimination of counterproductive bureaucratic procedures • Introduction of better lighting, sound buffers to decrease ambient noise, healthy air flow, and ergonomic furniture • Creation of networks to share knowledge and equipment	
Elimination of task interferences	The work environment creates conflicting priorities, and/or requires execution of activities that may decrease performance on essential tasks. As an example, filling out sales and contact reports may decrease time with customers and, hence, sales.	• Setting up of work priority sheets with a procedure and facilitative verification and approval process • Assignment of tasks to individuals most capable and desirous of performing these while freeing up others to focus on remaining required tasks • Auditing of tasks being performed and elimination or reassignment of nonessential/inappropriate ones • Policy setting that rewards accomplishment of priority tasks • Automation of routine tasks • Removal of trivial tasks from key workers	

Environmental intervention	Description/explanation	Sample applications	Application in my setting
Selection	Persons who do not have essential prerequisite skills and knowledge or appropriate characteristics and talents to perform drain the organization's resources. Training may improve performance somewhat, but will rarely achieve desired results. The negative consequences to the individual, work colleagues, and customers can be dramatic and costly when selection is inappropriate.	• Establishment of competency and characteristics that are requirements for the job along with performance-based measures for selection • Creation of a performance-based assessment center • Setting of clear performance goals (both behaviors and accomplishments) with predetermined check-points during a specified trial period • Targeted recruitment to the widest range of high-probability sources for appropriate candidates • Training of selection committee members on performance-based selection and provision of clear examples of poor selection—with consequences	
Provision of support	Performance, especially during early stages, requires encouragement, monitoring, and support. Research shows that when early performance attempts fail, individuals become discouraged and soon return to previous patterns of behavior or give up.	• Creation of initial meetings that cooperatively define performance expectations • Encouragement and rewards for initial performance attempts • Building of regular monitoring and support systems that include coaching • Creation of a performance tracking system with specific supervisor intervention menus • Recognition and publicizing of accomplishments • Scheduling of regular meetings to review performance and provide support • Provision of adequate resources to demonstrate support	

The interventions listed in the worksheet are but a few of the many possibilities that can range from business process reengineering and increased empowerment to ergonomics and wellness interventions. (Yes. More and more organizations are creating health and fitness programs to address a range of physical and mental well-being issues that can seriously affect performance and absenteeism. This is growing in importance as the workforce ages and workplace pressures increase.)

In our own work, we have applied all of the interventions listed in Worksheet 8-3, in some cases many times, to help improve performance. Here are some examples:

- **Provision of information**—In a hospital with rising postoperative infections, by providing weekly reports in the form of graphs showing infection rates for the hospital overall and for each individual department concerned (e.g., oncology, orthopedics, cardiology, obstetrics/gynecology), infection rates decreased 30 percent over a six-week period. Also, in the banking industry, by providing to loan officers weekly "success cases" along with contact information in selling new economy loans, this new type of complex loan—a major initiative for the bank—increased more than 600 percent over a one-year period. (Other interventions were also used.)

- **Provision of resources**—The provision of additional printers in a procurement department led to speedier decision making and reporting. Imagine. In a company with a procurement budget of more than $16 billion, procurement specialists had to share printers—four to a printer. And in a construction environment where women were being increasingly introduced into jobs in well-paying trades, accidents and injuries were significantly higher for the women. Redesign and distribution of safety gear to fit women's proportions and requirements dramatically decreased safety and injury incidents.

- **Redesign of work environment**—Increased sound absorbing baffles installed around each workstation and a much upgraded telephone system greatly improved customer service in an insurance company's newly created centralized customer service center. In another company, elimination of forms to be filled out to obtain safety gear and completely free access by workers to the equipment (formerly under guard and distributed by a clerk upon receipt of a filled-out form) increased safety gear use by 30 percent. In the first three months of monitoring the redesigned system, there were no incidents of safety gear theft or misuse.

- **Elimination of task interferences**—The Harry's Diner case you have encountered in earlier chapters provides an example of how elimination of tasks such as filling salt shakers, setting tables during busy periods, and bathroom checks can improve toast-serving performance. In the pharmaceutical sales arena, by eliminating or reducing and streamlining certain tasks such as territory planning, contact reporting, organizing of educational meetings, book report writing, and attendance and participation at numerous meetings, pharmaceutical representatives increased their number of doctor visits significantly.

◆ **Selection**—Did you notice what the prime selection criterion for ticket agents was in the public transit case illustrating the use of a matrix job aid to help sell monthly passes? Please write it here.

If you wrote down "former bus driver" or something similar, then it must have struck you as strange, although very humane. Here is an obvious case where the selection system is not aligned with the job (but does create good union-management relations). One of our most interesting performance improvement cases dealt with engineering design teams that were having trouble functioning properly and were not meeting milestone deadlines. The request was for team-building training. Analysis suggested another path. While team members were chosen for their technical competencies, no attention was paid to personal characteristics. By altering team selection criteria to include this critical dimension, the result of putting together more compatible teams was reduced friction and more frequent on-time deliveries.

◆ **Provision of support**—In chapter 7, this issue was raised in dealing with transfer and Ivan's typing. When the Canadian railway system changed 45 percent of their operating rules, many thousands of railway dispatchers, locomotive engineers, shop workers, maintenance-of-way personnel, and others had to be recertified on these rules. However, once trained and certified on the new ways, months in advance of launch date, they were not permitted to use them—not until the stroke of midnight, December 9, when everyone had to start afresh with the new rules. The expectation was that "incidents" would rise dramatically because of the changes. One railway selected 100 top performers, trained them as trainers to help certify its 13,500 railway workers. They then held weekly refresher sessions until launch time, whereupon, these same 100 top performers rode the rails, worked with all groups to apply the new rules, and provided 24/7 support to all for six weeks following launch. The amazing result was a dramatic decrease in incidents from normal occurrences. Cost savings in avoidance of investigations, mishaps, and fines as well as avoidance of accidents more than made up for additional support costs.

The purpose of recounting these examples is to inspire you and trigger ideas for improving performance through environmental interventions in your own work environment. If you have come up with new ideas, return to Worksheet 8-3 and note these in the fourth column where appropriate.

EMOTIONAL INTERVENTIONS

This subcategory of nonlearning interventions includes incentives, consequences, and enhancement of motivation. Incentives are stimulus elements the environment provides that, when perceived as meaningful and valued, increase motivation to perform. Consequences are somewhat akin to incentives but occur after performance. Often these are only discovered once performance is complete. For example, upon cleaning up your office, a person you admire walks in and compliments its look and cleanliness. This is an unanticipated consequence. Breaking a rule where notice of punishments has been posted is an example of an anticipated consequence. Incentives are always known because they are announced beforehand.

Motivation is an internal state and is a response to external events. It is greatly influenced by three key factors:

- *Value*—how highly a person values the desired performance. The more highly he or she values it, the greater the motivation.
- *Confidence*—how strongly a person feels she or he will be successful in performing. Under- or overconfidence lowers motivation. The optimal motivating state is one of challenge along with an expectation of success through applied effort.
- *Mood*—a person's emotional state when required to perform. The more positive the mood the more motivated. Workplace conditions and climate affect mood.

Worksheet 8-4 presents interventions of an emotional nature along with descriptions/explanations and sample applications. A fourth column offers you space to note down ideas of how you can apply these interventions to your work setting.

Application of these interventions from our own and our colleagues' files are:

- **Provision of incentives/consequences**—The target was a significant increase in customer satisfaction scores for a customer service call center. Scores had been declining for several reasons (e.g., increased turnover, pressure to improve productivity, product changes). Agents believed that speed of call handling was the criterion for success. Management was pushing for a "values" change. In the intervention, agents were heavily consulted about what constituted fair and equitable

Worksheet 8-4. Emotional Interventions

Emotional intervention	Description/explanation	Sample applications	Application in my setting
Provision of incentives/consequences	People perform well when they see what is in it for them as well as for the organization. Clear, meaningful, equitable rewards for performance and consequences for lack of performance result in improved performance. Incentives may be both monetary and nonmonetary (e.g., trips, merchandise, time off). It is essential that the incentive/consequence systems be seen as fair—no rewards for inadequate performance and applies equally to all.	• Pay-for-performance system • Bonuses for outstanding achievements • Realignment of commissions on sales • Career enhancement opportunities • Recognition for superior performance • Enhanced status system (e.g., titles, pins) • Enhanced privileges • Positive reports placed in file • Time off • Additional resources provided • Increased responsibility and authority • Better workspace or furniture	
Enhancement of motivation	People perform better when motivated. Operationally, this means that they value what they do (or if not the task, then the reward attached to it), feel secure in their work, yet are challenged by it and believe that with reasonable effort they can achieve success.	• Value of required performance shown through meaningful explanation of impact • Links established between performance and personal growth • Unnecessary threats to job security eliminated • Desired performance made challenging yet attainable (through, for example, documented success cases by fellow workers) • Meaningful contests that stimulate self-challenge • Impact of performance on personal career made clear • Support systems that build confidence	

expectations/standards of performance. They also contributed to the creation of a rewards menu that ranged from money to merchandise, workspace decoration, time off, free lunches, group celebrations, and even increased work responsibilities. The implementation was done with care and employee involvement. The result was a steady and significant customer satisfaction score increase and an even greater surge in employee satisfaction (which research has shown to impact strongly on customer loyalty).

♦ **Enhancement of motivation**—Bus drivers see themselves as having two major responsibilities: driving the bus safely and meeting the schedule of stops. "Softer" aspects of the job leave them cold or even negative. When the public transit authority announced a new program emphasizing customer service and managing diversity aboard buses, reactions of drivers and their union were negative to outright hostile. Creating planning and problem-solving meetings involving drivers and union representatives along with community leaders and government officials created initial ties. Showing data on correlations between ridership decline and decreasing customer satisfaction (resulting in driver job losses) increased the "value" of these soft-skill areas. Further examination of demographic statistics showing that the highest bus ridership growth potential lay with the ethnically diverse populations, and social events mixing drivers with various community representatives further enhanced motivation to improve performance. Over a four-month period following initiation of the program, customer satisfaction scores climbed and negative incidents declined significantly.

Once again, these examples are provided to stimulate your own ideas, which we encourage you to note in Worksheet 8-4.

Putting It All Together

Table 8-1 brings together all of the intervention types presented in this chapter. It is also helpful in sorting out how and when each of these interventions might be used and with what benefits.

 Remember This

Once again, it's review time. Select the appropriate option in each of the following statements.

1. A professional who acts as a performance consultant (has to/does not have to) develop all the interventions he or she recommends.
2. A performance intervention (must provide a complete solution/may be part of a basket of solutions) to a performance problem.

Table 8-1. Performance Interventions: Putting It All Together

If your analysis indicates that performers cannot achieve desired results because they...	then select...	such as...	that offers...
do not have the necessary skills and knowledge	a learning intervention	natural experience	real-life trial-and-error learning.
		experiential learning	real-life learning with structured reflection.
		on-the-job training	informal learning guided by co-workers.
		structured-on-the-job training	organized and certified learning guided by trained lead workers.
		simulation	learning through realistic, but not real practice.
		role play	emotional learning (how it feels) through intense participation in realistic scenarios.
		laboratory training	learning from hands-on practice with real objectives and equipment.
		classroom training	learning from an instructor and peers with some practice as feasible.
		self-study	learning on one's own from structured resources.

(continued on page 132)

Table 8-1. Performance Interventions: Putting It All Together (continued)

If your analysis indicates that performers cannot achieve desired results because they...	then select...	such as...	that offers...
do not have the necessary skills and knowledge, but must still produce immediate, near-expert performance	a nonlearning intervention that acts as an external memory or expert guide	job aids	immediate performance of a highly specific nature once use of the job aid has been mastered. Predictable results.
		performance support system	sophisticated, expert or near expert performance once use of the performance support system has been mastered.
have a work environment that lacks facilitating elements or presents barriers to achieving desired performance	a nonlearning environmental intervention	provision of information	clear expectations, feedback, and access to unambiguous, required data and guidelines.
		provision of resources	tools, procedures, processes, time, and support needed to perform.
		work environment redesign	supportive physical, administrative, management, communication, and work-task structures that enhance performance.
		elimination of task interferences	clear focus on priority tasks and results and suppression or reassignment of nonessential activities.

If your analysis indicates that performers cannot achieve desired results because they...	then select...	such as...	that offers...
have a work environment that does not stimulate, encourage, or reward desired performance or in which performers do not demonstrate an interest to perform as desired	a nonlearning emotional intervention to build commitment, engagement, and perseverance to perform	selection	the right performers for the job in terms of competencies, characteristics, and values.
		provision of support	people, systems, and structures that foster increasingly greater performance through encouragement, monitoring, feedback, and reward.
		provision of incentives/consequences	tangible monetary or nonmonetary rewards that performers value for performing as desired or recognition for valued rewards.
		enhancement of motivation	increased perception of value with respect to desired performance, appropriate level of confidence to succeed, and positive feelings toward achievement of valued results.

3. A performance intervention (may include/may not include) removal of an obstacle that prevents performance from occurring.
4. The learning intervention category (includes/does not include) job aids and performance support systems.
5. Psychodramas and sociodramas are examples of (simulation/role play).
6. To help increase bank tellers' accuracy in deciding whether to cash a check presented at the counter, you could design (a job aid/an incentive system).
7. Workers have clear expectations of desired performance. However, they are still confused about how well they are performing. You would recommend (clearer procedures/clearer feedback).
8. Despite well-designed and well-delivered training and a very supportive environment with excellent processes and tools, the new batch of workers is not achieving desired work results as previous groups have. You might suspect this situation requires (reexamining the selection system/refresher training).
9. (Incentives/Consequences) are offered prior to performance; (incentives/consequences) occur as a result of performance.
10. Overconfidence can lead to (increased/decreased) performance.

Please examine the feedback for each of the statements.

1. A professional who acts as a performance consultant does not have to develop all the interventions he or she recommends. As we've frequently mentioned, performance consulting requires teamwork. You should be able to build excellent relationships with your clients and be highly competent in analyzing performance issues. You should also have excellent selling/convincing capabilities to influence your clients in making sound performance decisions. You don't have to be capable of designing and developing all the interventions. That's what your team of resources is for.

2. A performance intervention may be part of a basket of solutions to a performance problem. Rarely does a single intervention work. Think systemically.

3. A performance intervention may include removal of an obstacle that prevents performance from occurring. In some ways, this is the best type of intervention. Removing obstacles is often less expensive than building something new. Always look to eliminate barriers whenever possible.

4. The learning intervention category does not include job aids and performance support systems. These are suitable interventions where there is a lack of skills and knowledge, just like learning interventions. However, job aids and performance support systems are substitutes for learning. They replace acquisition of competencies with virtually instant expert performance. They are a quick response where it is not necessary or feasible for performers to acquire the necessary expertise.

5. Psychodramas and sociodramas are examples of role play. They center on feelings and attitudes. They deal with emotions and trigger insights. Simulations are dynamic representations of systems. They are used to help learners acquire knowledge of how the system works, identify how elements interrelate, and build skills in manipulating and controlling the system elements and their functioning.

6. To help increase bank tellers' accuracy in deciding whether or not to cash a check presented at the counter, you could design a job aid. They come in different forms, one of which is a decision table. It lays out, in table format, the range of possible occurrences (e.g., if a customer requests cash for a check less than $50 and has an account with our branch, then verify ID and signature and cash the check) for easy decision making. Incentive systems are used to increase desire to perform, which in this instance is hardly relevant. Bank tellers generally want to cash checks correctly because this is an essential part of the job.

7. Workers have clear expectations of desired performance. However, they are still confused about how well they are performing. You would recommend clearer feedback. If performers are uncertain of their performance, feedback is lacking. Clearer procedures may help them perform better, but not inform them of results (unless this type of information is included as part of the procedure; it would then be called "feedback").

8. Despite well-designed and well-delivered training and a very supportive environment with excellent processes and tools, the new batch of workers is not achieving desired work results as previous groups have. You might suspect this situation requires reexamining the selection system. If it has all worked before and nothing has changed except for "the new batch of workers," verify the selection process and criteria. If training did not succeed a first time, "refresher training" is unlikely to be the answer.

9. Incentives are offered prior to performance; consequences occur as a result of performance.

10. Overconfidence can lead to decreased performance. It translates into lack of attention, lower value attribution, and increased error rate. The result, whether in identifying dangerous situations or starting up a piece of equipment, can be devastating.

You now possess an extensive intervention menu and the information and tools for improving performance. The next chapter presents more on how you, as a key player, can make it work. It focuses on the range of competencies and characteristics you will probably want to possess over time.

Making It Happen

Chapter Highlights:

- ◆ Key performance consulting competencies
- ◆ Critical performance consulting characteristics
- ◆ How to build trust, credibility, and partnerships

Whether you realize it or not, if you've traveled this far in *Training Ain't Performance*, you have become a performance consultant. You have adopted a performance perspective and acquired an operational model, a diagnostic process, and an impressive repertoire of performance interventions. You're getting ready to set up shop, if you haven't already done so. What more do you require? Certainly, competencies to make it all happen.

Building Professional Performance Consulting Competencies

To build required competencies, you first have to define the field of endeavor in which you're involved. Let's do this in four steps:

Performance: Human accomplishment, the valuable output of behavior, the execution and accomplishment of work.

Consulting: The range of activities applied to change or improve a situation without having direct control over the implementation.

Consultant: A person in a position to have some influence over an individual, a group, or an organization, but who has no direct power to make changes or implement programs.

Performance Consultant: A professional whose mission is to help engineer systems that result in human accomplishments, which are valued by the organization and its stakeholders.

We have borrowed liberally from several sources to build the preceding definitions. They all lead right to you. If your mission is to obtain the best performance possible from people in your workplace, but you can only accomplish this through influence rather than direct control, then you are a performance consultant. Do you feel competent and confident to carry out the mission?

- ☐ **Yes**
- ☐ **No**
- ☐ **Uncertain**

You probably should have checked off the "uncertain" box because you already have a lot of what it takes to do the job, but realize there's much more to acquire to become fully competent.

Two Broad Sets of Competencies

Performance consultants require two sets of competencies: technical and people. Examine each of these:

Technical: This set of competencies includes observation and analysis, design, and technology and media knowledge.

People: This includes skills in management and communication and interpersonal skills.

The two sets of competencies intertwine and apply across a broad range of activities you perform when you set out to make performance happen. Worksheet 9-1 lists more specifically the competency areas you require to become a strong performance consultant. As you read each one, check off whether you feel competent, you're working on it, or this is new for you and you'll have to learn more about it. As you discovered in chapter 6 on the various roles you can play, you will find here that you already possess many relevant strengths, but still have lots of room for growth and development.

Worksheet 9-1. Performance Consulting Competency Areas

Competency area	I feel competent.	I'm working on it.	This is new for me. I'd better learn more.
1. Determine performance improvement projects appropriate to work on.	☐	☐	☐
2. Conduct performance gap analyses.	☐	☐	☐
3. Assess performer characteristics.	☐	☐	☐
4. Analyze the structures of jobs, tasks, and content.	☐	☐	☐
5. Write statements of performance intervention outcomes.	☐	☐	☐
6. Analyze the characteristics of a learning/working environment.	☐	☐	☐
7. Sequence performance intervention outcomes.	☐	☐	☐
8. Specify performance improvement interventions and strategies.	☐	☐	☐
9. Sequence performance improvement activities.	☐	☐	☐
10. Determine resources appropriate for performance improvement activities and help obtain these.	☐	☐	☐
11. Evaluate performance improvement interventions.	☐	☐	☐
12. Create a performance improvement implementation plan.	☐	☐	☐
13. Plan, manage, and monitor performance improvement projects.	☐	☐	☐
14. Communicate effectively in visual, oral, and written form.	☐	☐	☐
15. Demonstrate appropriate interpersonal, group-process, and consulting skills.	☐	☐	☐
16. Promote performance consulting and human performance improvement as a major approach to achieving desired results in organizations.	☐	☐	☐

Where you placed your checkmarks should give you a quick portrait of how well prepared you are to deal with what it takes to obtain performance from people, which ultimately links to achieving business results. Don't be discouraged if you have discovered you still have a lot to learn. Take this as a positive sign of how rich the field of endeavor is that you have joined.

Performance Consulting Characteristics

Competencies are necessary, but not sufficient to make performance happen. You also need certain characteristics that can help you influence clients and decision makers. We interviewed 20 top performance improvement specialists. These individuals are recognized leaders in the field, have practiced the profession for some 20 to 50 years, and are all published authors on various aspects of workplace performance. We then distilled their wise counsel down to 10 key characteristics. Worksheet 9-2 lists these with some additional detail. Evaluate yourself against these items. Also, have someone you respect and trust rate you on these. Compare results and discuss similarities and differences of perception. This will make for a very useful dialogue and help you gain insights into your personal traits related to performance improvement.

In your self-evaluation you should discover where your strengths are and which characteristics you still have to work on. If you checked off any "This is beyond me" items, seriously question whether this is truly so. In our experience, it is rare to find a person concerned with achieving valued business accomplishments who really doesn't possess the 10 characteristics. If any items remain after serious reflection, then when the particular characteristic is required, turn to colleagues and team members for support.

Building Credibility and Trust

Your title includes the word "training" and/or your group is called "training . . . ." Why then should anyone believe that you do anything other than training? You have evolved. How do you get your clients to evolve with you?

The answer, fortunately, is relatively simple. Before making the grand announcement that you or your group has become the "learning and performance support" organization, build credibility and trust with clients and stakeholders. Here are six steps that others have taken to achieve success.

1. *Find a friendly, open client who is very much focused on performance and who has a situation that offers a high probability of success.* Go for something relatively simple and certain to result in clear performance improvements. It should be one that requires more than one intervention other than training. Partner with the client. Establish bottom-line metrics—key performance indicators that you can measure. Conduct your analysis, identify, develop, and help implement the interventions. Monitor results. Collect data. Write up the case.

Worksheet 9-2. Performance Consulting: Critical Characteristics

Characteristics	Yes, that's me.	I have to improve this.	This is beyond me.
1. Focused on client need. • Never loses sight of the primary mission: determines what will produce optimal performance. • Not swayed by enthusiasms or constraints. • Separates wants and whims from real needs. • Sticks to valued outcomes despite pressures.	☐	☐	☐
2. Cause-conscious, not solution-oriented. • Analytic. • Systematic investigator.	☐	☐	☐
3. Able to maintain a system perspective. • Adopts a holistic view. • Anticipates how change in one area affects others.	☐	☐	☐
4. Capable of involving others (authority figures, knowledgeable individuals) appropriately. • Stresses complementary skills. • Draws strength from team diversity.	☐	☐	☐
5. Organized, rigorous, and prudent. • Lets credible data talk.	☐	☐	☐
6. Sensitive of the need to verify perceptions. • Does reality checks with reliable persons. • Double (even triple) checks interpretations.	☐	☐	☐
7. Able to sort out priorities. • Focuses on and sticks to business needs. • Avoids technology seduction.	☐	☐	☐
8. Diplomatic and credible. • Convincing. • Overcomes resistance without creating antagonism.	☐	☐	☐
9. Generous with giving credit to others. • Highlights others' accomplishments. • Shares in rewards and recognition of success.	☐	☐	☐
10. Principled yet flexible. • Sticks to the bottom-line goal. • Bends to pressures and constraints without giving up the goal. • Accommodates client wants where and when feasible without losing sight of the desired result.	☐	☐	☐

2. *Conduct "show and tell" events.* Hold a free lunch to which you invite clients and other influential persons. During the lunch, show success stories. Have the client or clients with whom you have had success do much of the presenting. Demonstrate, with data, the value of your performance approach.

3. *Circulate information about the new services you offer and invite inquiries.* Just as external vendors do, market your expanded repertoire of services. Create a brochure. Circulate brief articles that support your approach. (ISPI and ASTD publications are excellent sources.) Write up success stories for internal newsletters. Share authorship with your clients.

4. *Offer to participate in business initiatives that will require performance change before you are asked to provide training.* Get there early so that you can act strategically to influence decisions before they are imposed on you. Offer a unique perspective on people performance.

5. *Change your department name and/or job title.* Obtain champion assistance and work with your group to create a new title and image that fits your new mission. Include "performance" in it.

6. *Build your competencies.* Evaluate your current and desired competencies. Create development programs and activities that will carry you and your team beyond training to performance.

Building Partnerships

To achieve performance success for yourself and your team, you must create powerful partnerships. The three critical ones are with clients, internal others, and external others.

Client partnerships. This partnership is the most crucial for success. Clients often view training groups as order-takers. "Here's my problem. Now fix it with training." Your new mission requires that you let your clients know:

- You can do more for them than just training.

- You can add much greater value and probably save money and time if you are permitted to work "with" rather than "for" them.

- You care about their overall business success and want to share in the challenge and responsibility.

Take a client to lunch. Discuss his or her issues. Speak the client's language (i.e., business not training). Demonstrate your desire and capability to be a partner in the effort and outcome. Underscore the key benefits: focus on their performance (not just learning) needs, sharing of expertise, possible time and cost savings, measured results, ongoing support, shared responsibility in the effort, and results.

Developing deep, lasting client partnerships takes time and must be continually renewed. These partnerships should be long term. The rewards for this type of relationship are many: higher probability of making significant, demonstrable contributions to client and business success; earlier involvement in projects; richer basket of interventions; greater respect and status; stronger influence on what counts; career development and growth.

Partnerships with internal others. Achieving performance success requires the assistance, collaboration, and support of many persons and groups outside of your own. Here is a partial list of potential partners: organizational development (OD) specialists, organizational effectiveness (OE) specialists, information technology (IT) groups, evaluation specialists, communication groups, ergonomics specialists, media specialists, financial experts, content specialists. Depending on projects, it is very useful to be able to call on these diverse internal resources to add depth to what you are trying to accomplish for your clients. What's in it for these internal partners is a break from the routine, a chance to make unique and significant contributions, and an opportunity to learn something new and to gain recognition for their contributions. At some future time, they can also call on this internal partner network for assistance. Their support in your venture can only enhance your credibility, trust, and success.

Partnerships with external others. Successful learning and performance support groups build banks of trusted, reliable outside partner-providers who can come aboard quickly and seamlessly to join in performance improvement projects. You seek out quality providers, verify capabilities, and place them in a preferred database. The benefits of creating these external partnerships are their rapid learning curve, proven capability, trusted relationship, seamless integration with you and your team, and that they come at a cost only when used. These partners, generally highly expert in their own areas of performance improvement, add to your own performance success. You can also learn a great deal from them. Usual external partners include performance analysts, intervention design and development specialists (e.g., compensation, human factors, workflow design), media and technology specialists, and evaluation specialists.

Building Consulting Expertise

Because there are so many books and other resources on consulting, other than to send you to the For Further Reading section at the back of this book there is little we can add. What we can do here is summarize several essential points.

Consulting is a process of building a relationship; identifying needs; sharing expertise; recommending appropriate, economical, feasible, acceptable interventions; and helping translate all of this to successful results for your client and the organization.

An excellent consulting engagement is based on creating credibility and trust, which results in your ability to influence those who are the decision makers and hold the levers of power.

How you achieve consulting success is through the following:

- **Listen actively and completely.** Immerse yourself in your client's issues and concerns. Listen beyond the words to the deeper meanings. Do your homework beforehand; learn about your client, the organization he or she represents, and key issues. Hear what is being said. Record (in writing) what your client tells you. This shows respect for the client's words and helps you focus on and retain important points.

- **Ask a lot of open-ended questions.** The client may come to you with a request. Offer reassurance that you can "solve the problem," and then drive toward the business need and the human performance requirements. Examine the brief case below.

Case: Better Communication

Call Center Director (CCD): . . . and so we've got to get the supervisor and team leads better trained on how to communicate with their customer service agents.

Performance Consultant (PC): I can help you solve this problem. I'd really like to understand the issue thoroughly so that I can best be of service. Can you tell me more?

CCD: Our customer service agent turnover is way too high. And our exit interviews inform us that the problem often lies with the supervisor.

PC: In what way?

CCD: The complaint is that supervisors and team leads don't provide enough support, especially early on when we get our biggest washout and turnover. When there's a problem, they don't seem to listen or are in a hurry. They answer that the standards are there for all to follow. They show no flexibility when an agent has a personal problem.

PC: If everything were working perfectly, what would be different? What would the most important change be?

CCD: Well, the most important change would be dramatically reduced agent turnover. That would save us millions of dollars and improve customer service. That's why I'm asking you for the communication course for supervisors and team leads.

Examine all the questions the performance consultant asked. What do you notice? Check off the statements that match your perceptions.

- ☐ 1. **All the questions are open-ended. They lead to elaboration of the need.**

- ☐ 2. **The questions focus on how best to deliver the communication course.**

☐   3.   **The questions try to probe beyond the client request to determine the business need.**

☐   4.   **The questions try to identify supervisor and team lead weaknesses.**

If you carefully studied the questions the performance consultant asked, you probably noticed that they were all open-ended questions. Their purpose was to find out more about the real business need (1, 3, and 4). Asking such questions requires conscious effort. The result is that soon you have the client moving away from the original request and talking to you about the real issues. At this point, you are no longer the order-taker, but a consultant.

- ◆ **Filter, direct, probe.** An essential part of consulting is getting beyond the surface. Most often, clients view us in a certain role and then pitch their words in light of their perceptions. If we are "trainers," they talk about training to us. If they see us as performance problem solvers and partners, their discourse changes. The successful consultant filters out the surface words, directs the client toward root issues, and tirelessly (but diplomatically) probes until the ultimate concerns are articulated. A benefit of this consultative approach, similar to what often happens in therapy, is that the client comes up with what is really needed, thus becoming more open to a basket of performance interventions. The client comes to realize that the training alone won't lead to performance.

- ◆ **Confirm that you have understood and are on the right track.** Periodically verify with your client that you understand the need. Along the way, keep the client informed of what you are discovering. Check and recheck—showing data whenever possible—to ensure that both the client and you are on the same wavelength.

- ◆ **Report.** You are in a partnership with your client. Keep him or her current with respect to what you are accomplishing. The best consulting relationships are ones that maintain open channels of communication. Let all stakeholders know what is going on without inundating them with details. Keep reports crisp and to the point.

- ◆ **Make the roadmap clear.** No surprises please. Keep your clients and stakeholders aware of future actions and timelines. If everyone knows where she or he is going, the probability is high that you will all get there.

Client Responsibilities and Ways You Can Assist

Making it happen depends on your competencies, characteristics, and consulting capabilities. Nevertheless, clients also have an important role to play. You can help them fulfill it. There are times when you are an extra pair of hands, just helping out your client by doing what she or he asks for. There may be other times when the client disappears, and you seem to have taken over, doing everything without him or her. While these happen from time to time, they mustn't occur too often. The ideal state of partnership for performance success is a collaborative one with shared responsibilities and duties.

Table 9-1 outlines client responsibilities for ensuring a performance improvement project's success, and what you can do to make sure your client engages in each of these. As you examine the table, imagine you are involved in a large-scale performance improvement project that includes not only you as the key performance consultant player, but also a team of internal and external resources.

Smaller-scale projects are not quite as demanding. Nevertheless, the principles embedded in the table apply. Clients must, at a minimum, approve, provide resources, monitor progress and results, and reward/reinforce. Your job remains one of being there to assist and facilitate as appropriate.

Reviewing the Key Points of "Making It Happen"

Your mission is business success through people performance. Your role is that of the partner consultant. Your job is to:

- Inform clients and stakeholders of what performance consulting is and is not (e.g., just training). To be successful, you must explain the roles and services they should expect from you. To do this, you will have to provide concrete examples.
- Show samples of what you and your learning and performance support team have done for other internal clients. Create and foster appropriate expectations as you transform from order-taker to the new, expanded, and organizationally vital performance improvement role.
- Explain what you mean by working in partnership with clients. Define the responsibilities clients retain during each phase of the performance improvement process. These generally include

  — Reviewing all performance analysis materials and reports
  — Reviewing identified interventions and their rationales and providing input on economics, feasibility, and organizational acceptability
  — Approving the final selection of performance interventions
  — Participating in resource selection or approving selected resources
  — Providing information and content expertise (personally or through appropriate specialists); facilitating access to required content information/subject matter experts

Table 9-1. Client Responsibilities and Ways You Can Assist

Client responsibilities	Ways you can assist
Approve analysis, selection, design/development, and implementation outputs (intermediate and final)	• Review reports and materials for approval prior to submission to the client • Verify that all reports and materials requiring client approval are clear and accompanied by credible rationales and data • Ensure sufficient lead time for client review and approval • Facilitate approval meetings • Mediate between client and performance team if there is lack of clarity or differences in understanding
Provide resources	• Determine reasonableness of resource requests prior to client submission • Coordinate resource requests • Identify and qualify resources beforehand • Help prepare rationales for resource requests • Identify alternative solutions to resource requests (e.g., simulations as opposed to early trials with actual performers)
Support performance improvement team	• Explain to client need for constant support to facilitate performance improvement team's work • Obtain authority to act on behalf of client • Schedule and facilitate periodic meetings with client to update him/her on progress and transmit support needs
Facilitate payments	• Inform client of payment issues and consequences • Prepare files on payment problems (e.g., delays in purchase orders or invoice processing) • Intercede with legal, accounting, or client payment processing to speed up payments
Contract	• Help prepare contracts and purchase orders for signature • Explain contract terms and invoicing requirements to contracted resources • Facilitate processing of contracts and purchase orders
Monitor progress and results	• Provide client with progress updates and implementation results • Create/build an ongoing evaluation system • Report meaningful data to client • Bring to client attention significant milestone achievements, problems, or data
Reward/reinforce	• Bring to client attention opportunities for recognition • Suggest appropriate means for recognition • Create recognition symbols and events

— Facilitating access to targeted performers for tryouts

— Participating in budget and timeline reviews

— Ensuring timely review of payment requests and payment to vendors

— Participating in planning, decision making, and, as appropriate, troubleshooting

— Providing feedback and reinforcement for successes.

♦ Guide clients to protect the performance improvement initiatives and team so that they may focus on critical tasks.

♦ Help clients to produce communications, activities, and showcases for accomplishments concerning their performance improvement efforts. Use these to inform senior management, other parts of the organization, and even the larger external communities. Help them to shine. Their success is your success.

Remember This

This chapter has provided you with a great deal of material to "make it happen." Here is a review to help retain some of the important points. Select from the alternatives presented in each of the following statements the one you feel is the better fit.

1. A performance consultant has (influence/control) over an individual, a group, or an organization, but has no direct (influence/control) to make changes or implement programs.

2. Performance consultants require two broad sets of competencies. These are (technical and people/training and client content knowledge).

3. If you discover that to transform yourself to become a performance improvement professional you have a lot to learn, this is a (negative/positive) sign.

4. An important characteristic of a performance improvement professional is to be able to be principled (and unyielding/yet flexible).

5. Announce that your group has become the "learning and performance support organization" (then build/only after you have built up) credibility and trust with clients and stakeholders.

6. To achieve performance success in yourself and your team, you must create powerful (control/partnerships).

7. A key benefit of building partnerships with external resources is (a rapid learning curve/organizational support).

8. In consulting, the more you ask open-ended questions and get the client to talk, the greater the chance that she or he will (move away from the original request and identify underlying business issues/become more committed to the original request).

9. An excellent performance consulting engagement is based on creating (excellent learning and development programs/credibility and trust).

10. As a performance consultant, you can (only assist with/fully take over) the client's responsibilities for a performance improvement project.

Compare your selections with ours.

1. A performance consultant has influence over an individual, a group, or an organization, but has no direct control to make changes or implement programs. Influence, based on credibility and trust, is the consultant's chief weapon. Control resides with management.

2. Performance consultants require two broad sets of competencies. These are technical and people. Performance consultants must be able to observe, analyze, design, develop, evaluate, and deal with technology. These are technical competencies. To ensure that a project succeeds, however, the performance consultant must also possess management, communication, and strong interpersonal capabilities. These are people competencies.

3. If you discover that to transform yourself to become a performance improvement professional, you have a lot to learn, this is a positive sign. Transformation doesn't have to be instantaneous. You already have a lot of the basics through your experience in training. Build from there. Grow in competence and confidence. What a wonderful road ahead of you!

4. An important characteristic of a performance improvement professional is to be principled yet flexible. Listen to clients and stakeholders. Bend where it won't affect the ultimate goal: desired performance. However, be careful in bending that you don't break and end up heading toward behavior without valued accomplishment.

5. Announce that your group has become the "learning and performance support organization" only after you have built up credibility and trust with clients and stakeholders. If you make your move too early, you may get blank stares and strong skepticism about your ability to perform. A much better strategy is to pave the way with accomplishments that build credibility and trust. Then, when your announcement comes, it will be no surprise.

6. To achieve performance success in yourself and your team, you must create powerful partnerships. The key is collaboration with clients, stakeholders, and both internal and external resources. Control is not the issue. Performance consulting works best in a partnered arrangement where all have a stake in the results.

7. A key benefit of building partnerships with external vendors is a rapid learning curve. If you identify quality external partners and use and reuse them, over time they almost become part of the organization. Their familiarity with the culture, issues, and people, even customers, reduces learning time. They become operational almost immediately.

8. In consulting, the more you ask open-ended questions and get the client to talk, the greater the chance that she or he will move away from the original request and identify underlying business issues. Ask questions that force the client to reveal what he or she hopes will be accomplished as a result of fulfilling the request. Probe for the bottom line—the business need. Your questioning can help the client clarify thoughts and even discover better ways to attain goals than what initially seemed the right way to go—probably the training default route.

9. An excellent performance consulting engagement is based on creating credibility and trust. This allows you to influence clients and stakeholders and obtain required resources. You may end up designing excellent learning and development programs that work and thus further enhance your credibility and trust. However, these do not form the basis of a consulting engagement. They are one of many possible outcomes.

10. As a performance consultant you can only assist with the client's responsibilities for a performance improvement project. The client is ultimately responsible for the accomplishments of her or his people. You help. You provide guidance, counsel, and resources. You assist the client in meeting responsibilities. Yet, the client retains authority and responsibility.

Another hefty chapter completed. You've certainly advanced along the performance path. You have a large toolkit with which to work and a considerable number of principles and guidelines to help you achieve performance success. Aha! "Performance success." What defines it? There are many different metrics from which you can select. One, however, stands out and is becoming an increasingly important preoccupation of senior managers—return-on-investment. If the organization is spending all this money to train and/or improve performance, what exactly is it getting for the considerable expenditure? How to answer? This is the subject of the next chapter.

Chapter 10

The Bottom Line: Demonstrating the Return-on-Investment of Your Interventions

Chapter Highlights:

◆ Calculating worth
◆ Calculating return-on-investment (ROI)
◆ Calculating payback period

Here is an actual scene one of us experienced. It took place in the office of the senior vice president of transportation (SVP) for a very large railway.

Case: Not Enough to Go Around

SVP: Look, I understand the need to train people and make them better at what they do. But, here's what I'm faced with. My transportation people tell me that they must have $100 million to upgrade our locomotives and purchase new ones. They've shown me a business case that demonstrates how much revenue we'll lose if we don't spend the money.

My information technology group tells me our systems are out of date, and we're falling behind the competition in tracking railway cars and shipments. They need $100 million to upgrade our systems. They've built a strong business case that really lays out both losses and gains depending on whether we invest in the upgrades.

Then there's the learning and performance group asking me for $50 million this year to upgrade competencies and improve people performance. But there's no business case! I don't have enough money for everything. If I don't invest in locomotives or computer systems, I know what will happen. You tell me what will happen if I don't invest in learning and performance for a year.

Performance Consultant: Uh . . .

Embarrassing, isn't it, to be standing in front of a key decision maker with no clear response? You need not be embarrassed in the future. In this chapter, you'll learn how to compete effectively for dollars in your organization.

You're in Competition

Money in organizations is scarce and getting scarcer as global competition forces everyone to become leaner and, unfortunately, meaner. Until relatively recently, training groups went about their activities unconcerned about the bottom line. Training was something necessary that organizations did. In the 1960s and 1970s, there was almost a golden age of training with a strong emphasis on "personal development." The tough economic period of the 1980s led to tighter reins on spending and greater demand for training accountability. In the 1990s, more emphasis was placed on tying training to improved productivity. This period also brought in a strong push to stretch beyond the narrow confines of training to a broader performance improvement paradigm. With this has also come a growing demand to demonstrate the worth of performance improvement interventions and return-on-investment in learning and performance.

The good news is that the last few years have produced resources that help us calculate and show worth and ROI. So here we are in the 21st century with competition for funds, demands to "show me the money," and means for doing just that.

Calculating Worth and ROI—It's Not So Hard

Many professionals in the learning and people development fields freeze when they hear "calculate ROI." Are you one of these?

- ☐ **Yes. I don't like/I'm not good at math.**
- ☐ **No. I don't mind doing calculations. Just show me how.**

Whether you responded "yes" or "no," we have good news for you. If you checked "yes," please note that all you have to do is add, subtract, multiply, and divide using a calculator. Surely you can do that. We've worked with hundreds of people like you, and they all survived and thrived. If you checked "no," you will find the process easy. A calculator, good data, and you're on your way.

First, a Few Preliminaries

The purpose of calculating worth and ROI is to help clients, decision makers, and stakeholders decide on whether to fund your performance improvement recommendations. Worth and ROI are financial concepts. Therefore, calculate these only when you can boil down performance outcomes (valued accomplishment) to economic terms.

Here is a list of desired outcomes. Check off those that you can see translate easily into valued accomplishments and on which you can place a monetary figure.

☐ 1. **Reduce wastage by 20 percent.**
☐ 2. **Increase the speed of ticket sales by 10 percent.**
☐ 3. **Eliminate all invoicing errors.**
☐ 4. **Improve presentation skills.**
☐ 5. **Write better proposals.**
☐ 6. **Improve customer satisfaction ratings.**
☐ 7. **Sell 100 more subscriptions per day.**
☐ 8. **Transform 10 percent of service calls to sales.**

This was a tough exercise. Numbers 1, 2, 3, 7, and 8 appear relatively obvious. Once you gather baseline information (e.g., wastage costs us $2,000 per day; therefore, 20 percent = $400), then you have an excellent starting place. Number 4, "improve presentation skills," is vaguer. In this case, you would have to probe. Perhaps you would discover that better presentation skills result in higher sales. By comparing high and low performers, you could arrive at a range of values for improved presentation skills. The same would hold true for number 6, "write better proposals." For number 7, "improve customer satisfaction ratings," you could turn to research or benchmarking firms that have data relating customer satisfaction scores by industry to revenues, customer retention, and actual monetary value.

The For Further Reading section contains books on this topic, and we recommend gaining greater depth from these in how you convert seemingly intangible outcomes to concrete numbers. In this chapter, we strongly suggest that you begin your calculation of worth and ROI adventures with relatively easy cases. This will build your competence and confidence. Once you have done some simpler ones, you'll be ready to stretch beyond these.

What Is Worth and ROI?

Worth, as we explained very early in this book, is a ratio of value (or benefit) to cost. The formula looks like this:

$$W = \frac{V}{C}$$

If the value in this ratio exceeds the cost of achieving it, then your performance interventions are worth it. Try these two examples. Decide in each case if it is worth it or not. You may use a calculator to help you.

1. The cost of training the field salesforce to sell the high-end printers, creating job aids and reference materials, and coaching and monitoring performance will be $60,000. Based on how our exemplary sales people are performing right now, high-end printer sales profits should improve by 25 percent. Our current profits from high-end printers are $600,000. Remember, W = V/C.

2. Samantha glared at the data. Customer satisfaction scores had dropped 7 percent over the last two quarters. Customer loss was 3 percent, resulting in lost revenues of $2,500,000, 40 percent of which represented lost profits. The performance improvement consultant was presenting her with a basket of interventions that would cost in total about $250,000—a lot of money in these tight times. Her team had worked with the consultant and was sure it would result in a complete recovery of the customer satisfaction score loss within six months. "Should I do it?" she asked herself. Again, remember the formula: W = V/C.

Let's calculate both of these cases.

1. Cost = $60,000

   Value = 0.25 x $600,000 = $150,000

   $$W = \frac{V}{C} = \frac{\$150,000}{\$60,000} = 2.5$$

   Thus, for each $1 invested, the printer company should obtain $2.50. The benefit-to-cost ratio is 2.5:1. Definitely worth it!

2. Cost = $250,000

   Value = 0.40 x $2,500,000 = $1,000,000

   $$W = \frac{V}{C} = \frac{\$1,000,000}{\$250,000} = 4$$

   For each $1 invested, Samantha should obtain $4 within six months. The benefit-to-cost ratio is 4:1. Do it, Samantha!

These two brief examples should illustrate for you the power of being able to calculate worth and the simplicity of the calculation itself.

Now, we turn it up a notch. As we said, worth is a benefit-to-cost ratio. For each dollar you spend, this is what you get. Return-on-investment presents a different type of information. It says, here's how much money you make once you take back your original investment. This requires that you subtract the cost (C) from the value (V) and, only then, divide by cost (C). To complete the calculation, multiply by 100 to get the ROI in percent. Let's see what this looks like.

1. The high-end printer case.

    Cost   = $60,000
    Value   = $150,000

$$ROI \;=\; \frac{V - C}{C} \times 100 \;=\; \frac{\$150{,}000 - \$60{,}000}{\$60{,}000} \times 100$$

$$=\; \frac{\$90{,}000}{\$60{,}000} \times 100$$

$$=\; 150$$

The ROI in this case is 150 percent. Great return!

2. The customer satisfaction score case.

    Cost   = $250,000
    Value   = $1,000,000

$$ROI \;=\; \frac{V - C}{C} \times 100 \;=\; \frac{\$1{,}000{,}000 - \$250{,}000}{\$250{,}000} \times 100$$

$$=\; \frac{\$750{,}000}{\$250{,}000} \times 100$$

$$=\; 300$$

The ROI in this case is 300 percent in six months. Wow!

These two cases are artificial, but, believe it or not, small performance improvements multiplied over many people make for huge ROIs. What powerful arguments to implement your performance improvement recommendations!

Now for the Real Stuff: Calculating ROI

The whole subject of ROI is very broad and can become increasingly technical. Despite this, you can still create strong "business cases" for your recommendations using the following guidelines. We have divided these into four parts: calculating costs, calculating value, calculating worth, and calculating ROI. We also show you how to calculate the payback period for an intervention.

CALCULATING COSTS

1. Start with all easily identifiable, major direct costs such as purchases, leases, and services related to the whole set of interventions. Don't forget nonrefundable taxes, transportation/installation/maintenance/insurance costs, and the like. Work with your purchasing and accounting specialists to get started.

2. For each intervention, calculate internal people hourly costs. You do this by obtaining their average annual base salaries (e.g., $50,000/year) and the number of days they work each year (subtract weekends, holidays, sick days, training days). Divide by the number of daily hours worked.

Example: Average salary = $50,000
Annual days worked = 220
Hours worked per day = 7.5

$$\text{Hourly cost} = \frac{\$50,000 \div 220}{7.5} = \$30.30$$

3. List each category of internal worker involved in each intervention. Here's a starter list. Check off those who are relevant. Note estimated number of hours for each category per intervention.

Hours			Hours		
_____	☐	**Instruction designers**	_____	☐	**Project managers**
_____	☐	**Developers**	_____	☐	**Internal consultants**
_____	☐	**Administrative personnel**	_____	☐	**Field personnel**
_____	☐	**Subject matter experts**	_____	☐	**Trainees**
_____	☐	**Desktop publishers**	_____	☐	**Coaches**
_____	☐	**Media specialists**	_____	☐	**Managers**
_____	☐	**IT personnel**	_____	☐	**Technical specialists**
_____	☐	**Trainers**	_____	☐	**Other:** _____

4. Multiply the number of hours by the average per-hour cost for each category of internal worker. Add these up to obtain a total.

5. Multiply the total internal people costs by:

   ◆ 1.0 if your organization counts only base salary costs.
   ◆ 1.5 for semiloaded costs (covers benefits, training, and other incidental costs).
   ◆ 3.0 for fully loaded costs that include the full cost of the organization's overhead attributed to each employee.

Example:

	Hours	x	Rate per hour ($)	=	Cost ($)
Instructional designers	225.00		30.30		6,817.50
Developers	150.00		27.50		4,125.00
Subject matter experts	60.00		35.00		2,100.00
Trainers	187.50		35.00		6,562.50
Project manager	300.00		39.30		11,790.00
Trainees	1,500.00		25.60		38,400.00
Managers (as coaches)	400.00		40.10		16,040.00
Desktop publisher	75.00		20.00		1,500.00
Total					87,335.00

Check company policy on how internal people costs are calculated and which factor to multiply by.

Example:

- Base salary only = $87,335 x 1.0 = $87,335.00
- Semiloaded costs = $87,335 x 1.5 = $131,002.50
- Fully loaded costs = $87,335 x 3.0 = $262,005.00

6. For each external worker:
    - Get hourly rates.
    - Multiply hourly rate by estimated number of hours for each intervention.
    - If work is at a fixed rate per project, get fixed rate.
    - Total all external people costs.

Example:

	Hours	x	Rate per hour ($)	=	Cost ($)
• Consultant	96		120		11,520
• Media specialist (fixed rate)					3,000
• Graphic artist	48		50		2,400
Total external people costs					16,920

7. For each intervention, calculate and total specific direct costs. Here's a starter list. Check off those that are relevant and insert costs. Add others as needed.

Costs		Costs	
_____ ☐ **Travel**		_____ ☐ **Facilities**	
_____ ☐ **Documentation**		_____ ☐ **Hotel**	
_____ ☐ **Printing**		_____ ☐ **Per diem**	
_____ ☐ **Media production**		_____ ☐ **Communications**	
_____ ☐ **Programming**		_____ ☐ **Courier/shipping**	
_____ ☐ **Specific purchases**		_____ ☐ **Other:** _____	

Example:	Cost ($)
Travel	8,000
Printing	2,000
Facilities (internal cost)	4,200
Hotel	2,400
Per diem	600
Courier/shipping	350
Total direct costs (training)	17,550

8. Calculate lost opportunity or replacement costs.

   ◆ Calculate revenues the organization will lose because someone involved in the project development or away at training as a result of the project is not generating revenues, and is not replaced.

   ◆ Calculate the cost of replacement for people who are working on the project, are being replaced while they are in training, or are in some way off the job because of the project.

9. Calculate maintenance cost.

   ◆ Calculate how much it would cost to update each intervention over the time period it will be used. Often you assign an estimated percentage of the development cost (e.g., if the intervention will be used for four years, it cost $200,000 to develop, and you estimate that maintenance costs may reach 10 percent of the initial intervention cost each year, then for years 2, 3, and 4, you add $20,000 each or a total of $60,000 for maintenance).

10. Add up the costs for all the interventions.

Example:

	Hours	x	Loss or replacement cost per hour ($)	=	Cost ($)
• Subject matter experts: lost opportunity	60		120.00		7,200
• Trainees	1,500		25.60		38,400
Total lost opportunity and replacement cost for the project					45,600

11. Add to the total for all the interventions the general costs such as general project management, administration, implementation, monitoring, and evaluation. This gives you your complete and total cost for the entire performance improvement project.

This looks like a lot of work. It may even appear complicated and difficult to do. Not so. Not if you take it a step at a time. On the next page is an example—a case, which we will follow through all the way to illustrate calculation of cost, value, worth, and ROI. We will even tack on at the end how long it will take to pay back all the costs of the project.

As you can see, once you obtain specific cost data, the calculations are not very difficult. You do have to track all costs—either estimated beforehand or actual after the fact. What is wonderful is that once you obtain people costs, which usually make up the bulk of the cost formula, you can reuse them in other projects. This is also true for certain direct costs related to facilities, shipping, and reproduction.

CALCULATING VALUE

 Before starting, it is extremely important that you estimate value in close collaboration with your client and/or credible subject matter specialists. We will repeat this caution in various calculation steps as we proceed. At the risk of being overly repetitive, your client and/or these specialists must commit to three important numbers: cost of an individual opportunity or deficiency, frequency of opportunities or deficiencies, and lowest and highest estimated percentage of impact of your interventions if you perform the calculation before you design and implement your interventions. Bear this in mind as we progress through the steps.

Case: Billing Errors—Calculating Costs

The internal auditor's report pointed out that billing errors made by clerks were costing the company anywhere from $4.5 to $13 million annually. Management's reaction to this, "Get those clericals trained to do their jobs right!" You did the analysis and presented a series of recommendations. Now you want to support your proposed performance improvement solutions with numbers. This is what you did by following the 11 steps we presented for calculating costs.

Eleven steps to calculate cost	Cost ($)
1. Cost of all purchases, leases, services related to the whole set of interventions	0.00
2. Calculation of cost of internal workers per intervention:	

Clerk: $26,000 ÷ 230 days = $113.04/day
                       $113.04 ÷ 8 hrs = $14.13/hr.

Team lead: $30,000 ÷ 230 days = $130.43/day
                       $130.43 ÷ 8 hrs = $16.30/hr.

Trainers: $40,000 ÷ 230 days = $173.90/day
                       $173.90 ÷ 8 hrs = $21.74/hr.

Managers/Project manager: $45,000 ÷ 230 days = $195.65/day
                       $195.65 ÷ 8 hrs = $24.46/hr.

3. Categories of workers and hours for each worker per intervention, **and**

4. Cost for each category or worker and total cost of all internal workers:

Category of worker	Rate per hour ($)	Hours	
Team Leads (also act as subject matter specialists)			
• Design	16.30	70	1,141.00
• Evaluation	16.30	20	326.00
Trainers			
• Delivery (8 hrs x 12 sessions)	21.74	96	2,087.04
• Preparation	21.74	24	521.76
Project manager			
• Project management	24.46	240	5,870.40
Clerks (8 hrs training time for 100 clerks)	14.13	800	11,304.00
Managers			
• Coaching (1 hr per clerk)	24.46	200	4,892.00
Total			26,142.20

5. Cost of all internal workers multiplied by 3 (fully loaded cost, which includes salary, benefits, and all overhead)—3 x $26,142.20   78,426.60

Eleven steps to calculate cost			Cost ($)
6. Cost of external workers:			
Category of worker	Rate per hour ($)	Hours	
Instructional designer			
• Training design	112.50	320	36,000.00
• Job aids design	112.50	32	3,600.00
• Coaching design	112.50	200	22,500.00
• Feedback system design	112.50	40	4,500.00
• Redesign of billing forms	112.50	64	7,200.00
Graphic designer			
• Training materials	40.00	64	2,560.00
• Job aids	40.00	32	1,280.00
• Coaching guides	40.00	32	1,280.00
• Feedback forms	40.00	16	640.00
• Billing forms	40.00	32	1,280.00
Programmer			
• Software redesign	110.00	80	8,800.00
• Feedback system	110.00	80	8,800.00
• Billing forms	110.00	48	5,280.00
• Debugging (all)	110.00	50	5,500.00
Total			109,220.00
7. Cost of all direct expenses:			
Production			
• All materials in final format			1,000.00
• Reproduction (training materials, job aids, reference materials, coaching guides)			7,000.00
• Facilities (internal charge $425 per group x 12 groups)			5,100.00
• Shipping			800.00
Total direct costs			13,900.00
8. Lost opportunity and/or replacement costs:			
• Not calculated since each clerk has four training days per year as part of the employment package. This is included in the number of workdays-per-year calculation.			0.00
9. Maintenance cost:			
• None; all training will take place over a four-month period.			0.00
10. Total cost for all interventions ($):			
• Internal workers		78,426.60	
• External workers		109,220.00	
• Direct costs		13,900.00	201,546.60
11. All overall costs attributed to intervention			0.00
Total cost of performance improvement solution			**201,546.60**

1. An opportunity is what is not yet being achieved. It is an individual occurrence of a gain that is being planned for. A deficiency is an individual occurrence of something that should be achieved but is not. State the lowest and highest individual opportunity or deficiency value. If this is an estimate, work with a credible specialist or team to define each of these. Your client and all stakeholders must believe these numbers.

lowest value = _____   **highest value = _____**

Example:

Transform a low-end to a high-end printer sale: profit value.

lowest value = _____$50_____   highest value = _____$100_____

---

2. State the lowest and highest frequency of occurrences for an individual opportunity or deficiency per worker per time period. (Usually you end up with a frequency per year.) If this is an estimate, then, as above, work with a credible specialist or team to determine these.

lowest frequency = _____   **highest frequency = _____**

Example:

Each salesperson serves about 50 to 60 customers per day. Each salesperson usually makes 5 to 10 sales a day.

lowest frequency = _____5/day_____   highest frequency = _____10/day_____

Each salesperson works 230 days per year, so annual lowest and highest sales frequencies are:

lowest frequency = _____1,150/year_____   highest frequency = _____2,300/year_____

---

3. Multiply the lowest and highest frequencies per worker by the total number of workers. This gives you the total number of opportunities or deficiencies per year (or specified time period).

lowest frequency x total workers = _____	highest frequency x total workers = _____

Example:

There are 60 salespersons in the company's stores.

$$\underline{1,150} \quad \text{x} \quad \underline{60} \quad = \underline{69,000} \quad \underline{2,300} \quad \text{x} \quad \underline{60} \quad = \underline{138,000}$$

| lowest frequency | total workers | highest frequency | total workers |

---

4. Multiply the lowest and highest individual opportunity or deficiency value from step 1 by the lowest and highest frequencies from step 3 to obtain the range of improvement values for a year (or the specified time period).

$$\underline{\hspace{3cm}} \quad \text{x} \quad \underline{\hspace{3cm}} \quad = \quad \underline{\hspace{3cm}}$$

| **lowest individual value** | **lowest total frequency** | **lowest value** |

$$\underline{\hspace{3cm}} \quad \text{x} \quad \underline{\hspace{3cm}} \quad = \quad \underline{\hspace{3cm}}$$

| **highest individual value** | **highest total frequency** | **highest value** |

Example:

$$\underline{\$50} \quad \text{x} \quad \underline{69,000} \quad = \quad \underline{\$3,450,000}$$

| lowest individual value | lowest total frequency | lowest value |

$$\underline{\$100} \quad \text{x} \quad \underline{138,000} \quad = \quad \underline{\$13,800.00}$$

| highest individual value | highest total frequency | highest value |

---

5. Multiply the lowest and highest values by the number of expected years the recommended performance interventions will have an impact.

_____	**x**	_____	**=**	_____
lowest value		**number of years**		**lowest total value**

_____	**x**	_____	**=**	_____
highest value		**number of years**		**highest total value**

Example:

$3,450,000	x	3	=	$10,350,000
lowest value		number of years		lowest total value

$13,800,000	x	3	=	$41,400,000
highest value		number of years		highest total value

---

6. Working with client experts, determine what would be the lowest and highest expected impact of your performance interventions on performance of the workers. Come up with credible, sensible estimates on both the low and high ends. (If you are using real value figures following implementation, you don't have to estimate. You work with one set of actual figures everywhere.) Multiply the lowest and highest total values by the lowest and highest percentage of impact.

_____	**x**	_____	**=**	_____
lowest total value		**lowest percentage of impact**		**lowest estimated value**

_____	**x**	_____	**=**	_____
highest total value		**highest percentage of impact**		**highest estimated value**

Example:

The credible low and high estimates of impact are 10% and 20%.

$10,350,000	x	0.10	=	$1,035,000
lowest total value		lowest percentage of impact		lowest estimated value

$41,400,000	x	0.20	=	$8,280,000
highest total value		highest percentage of impact		highest estimated value

According to these calculations, then, the estimated value the organization will receive if it adopts your basket of performance improvement interventions will range from the lowest to the highest estimated values—from $1,035,000 to $8,280,000.

To reinforce this calculation of value, let's apply the six steps to the Billing Errors Case for which we calculated costs of $201,547 back on pages 158-159.

Case: Billing Errors—Calculating Value

The order from management had been, "Get those clericals trained to do their jobs right!" Your translation of this imperative was, "Get those clericals to attain desired performance." You did your analysis, prescribed performance improvement interventions, and calculated the cost of these. Now to demonstrate value following the steps laid out above.

1. Show the lowest and highest individual deficiency value derived from the auditor's report.

$175	$300
lowest value	highest value

2. Show the lowest and highest frequency per worker.

5/week	10/week
lowest frequency	highest frequency

which turns into an annual frequency of (based on 230 workdays).

230/year	460/year
lowest frequency	highest frequency

(Each clerk generates approximately 40 invoices per day.)

3. Multiply lowest and highest frequencies per worker by the total number of workers (100).

230	X	100	= 23,000
lowest frequency		total workers	

460	X	100	= 46,000
highest frequency		total workers	

4. Multiply the lowest and highest individual deficiency value from step 1 by the lowest and highest frequencies in step 3. This gives you the range of improvement value for a year.

$175	X	23,000	=	$4,025,000
lowest individual frequency		lowest total frequency		lowest value

$300	X	46,000	=	$13,800,000
highest individual frequency		highest total frequency		highest value

(Continued on 166)

Case: Billing Errors—Calculating Value (continued)

5. Multiply the lowest and highest values by the number of expected years the recommended performance interventions will have an impact.

$$\underbrace{\$4,025,000}_{\text{lowest value}} \times \underbrace{3}_{\text{number of years}} = \underbrace{\$12,075,000}_{\text{lowest total value}}$$

$$\underbrace{\$13,800,000}_{\text{highest value}} \times \underbrace{3}_{\text{number of years}} = \underbrace{\$41,400,000}_{\text{highest total value}}$$

6. With client experts, determine lowest and highest expected impact on clerical performance. Multiply these by lowest and highest total value.

$$\underbrace{\$12,075,000}_{\text{lowest total value}} \times \underbrace{0.20}_{\substack{\text{lowest percentage} \\ \text{of impact}}} = \underbrace{\$2,415,000}_{\substack{\text{lowest estimated} \\ \text{value}}}$$

$$\underbrace{\$41,400,000}_{\text{highest total value}} \times \underbrace{0.30}_{\substack{\text{highest percentage} \\ \text{of impact}}} = \underbrace{\$12,420,000}_{\substack{\text{highest estimated} \\ \text{value}}}$$

For this case, the estimated value of your proposed interventions ranges from $2,415,000 to $12,420,000 over a three-year period.

CALCULATING WORTH

Remember, worth is the ratio of value to cost. Now that you have both total costs for your interventions and estimated lowest and highest values (or the actual value), the worth calculation is simple.

1. Start with your basic formula:

$$W = \frac{V}{C} \qquad \left[\text{Worth} = \frac{\text{Value}}{\text{Cost}} \right]$$

Create an equation for lowest value (V_L) and for highest value (V_H).

$$W_L = \frac{V_L}{C} \qquad W_H = \frac{V_H}{C}$$

Example (printer sales):

$$\mathbf{W_L} = \frac{V_L}{C} \qquad\qquad \mathbf{W_H} = \frac{V_H}{C}$$

$$= \frac{\$1,035,000}{\$201,546} \qquad\qquad = \frac{\$8,280,000}{\$201,546}$$

$$= 5.14 \qquad\qquad = 41.08$$

---

2. Express the result as a benefit-to-cost ratio:

$$W_L = \underline{\hspace{2cm}} : 1 \qquad W_H = \underline{\hspace{2cm}} : 1$$

Example (printer sales):

The lowest worth is 5.14:1; the highest worth is 41.08:1. This means that for each $1 invested, the organization can anticipate a benefit range of $5.41 to $41.08 over a three-year period.

The higher the ratio, the more it is worth to follow your recommendations.

CALCULATING ROI

The steps for calculating ROI are similar to those for worth. The key differences are that you first subtract cost from value before dividing by cost and the result is expressed as a percentage.

1. Start with your basic formula:

$$ROI_L = \frac{V_L - C}{C} \times 100 \qquad ROI_H = \frac{V_H - C}{C} \times 100$$

Example (printer sales):

$$\textbf{ROI}_L = \frac{V_L - C}{C} \times 100 \qquad \textbf{ROI}_H = \frac{V_H - C}{C} \times 100$$

$$\textbf{ROI}_L = \frac{\$1,035,000 - \$201,546}{\$201,546} \times 100 \qquad \textbf{ROI}_H = \frac{\$8,280,000 - \$201,546}{\$201,546} \times 100$$

$$= 414 \qquad\qquad\qquad\qquad = 4008$$

---

2. Express the result as a percentage:

$$ROI_L = \underline{\hspace{2cm}} \% \qquad ROI_H = \underline{\hspace{2cm}} \%$$

Example:

The lowest return-on-investment is 414% over three years and the highest is 4008%.

Often the ROI results are amazing. Small improvements in performance can yield very high returns.

CALCULATING PAYBACK PERIOD

Sometimes it is both helpful (and dramatic) to demonstrate how quickly the initial investment for creating and implementing all the interventions will be paid back. While the real calculations can actually become complicated, there is a simple formula for doing this. It offers a "lite" approach to calculating payback.

1. Start with the formula for a payback period:

$$PB = \frac{C}{V \div M}$$

$$Payback = \frac{Cost}{Value \div Number\ of\ Months}$$

Example:

If our project life is three years (36 months) of producing value totaling $1,000,000 to $2,000,000 and our costs are $250,000, then the calculation is:

$$PB_L = \frac{C}{V_L \div M} \qquad\qquad PB_H = \frac{C}{V_H \div M}$$

$$= \frac{\$250,000}{\$1,000,000 \div 36} \qquad\qquad = \frac{\$250,000}{\$2,000,000 \div 36}$$

$$= 9 \qquad\qquad\qquad\qquad\qquad = 4.5$$

---

2. Express the result as the number of months required to pay back the initial investment.

Example:

In this example, the payback period ranges from 4.5 months to 9 months. What a rapid payback in either case!

Please note that, usually, payback starts slowly before accelerating. For this reason, our formula is more of an indicator than an accurate statement. You would have to track monthly cash flow to obtain a truly accurate figure.

To conclude the Billing Errors Case and show how all the numbers come together, examine how worth, ROI, and payback period are calculated.

Case: Billing Errors—Calculating Worth, ROI, and Payback Period

1. $W_L = \dfrac{V_L}{C}$ $\qquad\qquad$ $W_H = \dfrac{V_H}{C}$

   $= \dfrac{\$2,415,000}{\$201,546}$ $\qquad\qquad$ $= \dfrac{\$12,420,00}{\$201,546}$

   $= 11.98$ $\qquad\qquad\qquad$ $= 61.62$

   The benefit-to-cost ratio ranges from 11.98:1 to 61.62:1. This means that for each $1 the organization invests, over a three-year period it will get benefits of $11.98 to $61.62. It's very much worth it to proceed.

2. $ROI_L = \dfrac{V_L - C}{C} \times 100$ $\qquad\qquad$ $ROI_H = \dfrac{V_H - C}{C} \times 100$

   $= \dfrac{\$2,415,000 - \$201,546}{\$201,546} \times 100$ $\qquad$ $= \dfrac{\$12,420,000 - \$201,546}{\$201,546} \times 100$

   $= 1098$ $\qquad\qquad\qquad$ $= 6062$

   Return-on-investment estimates range from 1098% to 6062%. Remarkable as these percentages are, these types of returns do occur when people performance improves across a large population.

3. $PB_L = \dfrac{C}{V_L \div M}$ $\qquad\qquad$ $PB_H = \dfrac{C}{V_H \div M}$

   $= \dfrac{\$201,546}{(\$2,415,000 \div 36)}$ $\qquad\qquad$ $= \dfrac{\$201,546}{(\$12,420,000 \div 36)}$

   $= 3$ $\qquad\qquad\qquad$ $= 0.58$

   In this fictitious example, the payback period for the money invested to develop and implement your recommended interventions ranges from a little over half a month to three months.

If the Billing Errors Case were real and the numbers were complete and accurate, even with a fully loaded cost of three times base salary, your proposed interventions would look very convincing—perhaps even too convincing. This is why we emphasize working with your client or client's experts to obtain the lowest and highest individual opportunity/deficiency value, the lowest and highest frequencies, and the lowest and highest estimated percentages of impact on performance.

A CONCLUDING NOTE ON CALCULATIONS

Talking numbers and calculations is not really fun. However, as you can see, showing high worth and ROI as well as rapid payback make for powerful arguments to clients and stakeholders. Be brave. Find a relatively straightforward case with which to start and go for it. You will find that it's not so difficult and the result is really convincing.

Remember This

Your head is probably reeling from the numbers. It will help to review the chapter and pull things together. Select from the alternatives the ones you feel best fit the statements that follow.

1. The learning and performance support organization (is/is not) in competition for funds with operational departments.
2. Calculating worth, ROI, and payback period (requires/does not require) math skills beyond addition, subtraction, multiplication, and division.
3. To calculate worth and ROI, it is (necessary/not necessary) to state performance outcomes in economic terms—hard numbers.
4. It is best to begin your calculating worth and ROI adventures with relatively (easy/complex) cases.
5. Worth is a (value expressed as a percentage/benefit-to-cost ratio).
6. ROI says here's how (long it will take to recoup/much money you will make as a percentage once you recoup) your original investment.
7. When calculating internal people's fully loaded costs, you multiply the base salary by (1.5/3).
8. The revenues or profits your organization does not earn because a person is in training and not doing his or her job is called (lost opportunity/replacement) cost.
9. In calculating value, it is essential to work with your (own/client's) team to estimate individual improvement values, frequencies, and percentage of impact on performance.
10. When estimating value, establish (a lowest to highest range/an average).

Now for feedback on your selections.

1. The learning and performance support organization is in competition for funds with operational departments. In this highly competitive global marketplace, everyone competes for funds. That's why you must be able to make a business case, just like everyone else.

2. Calculating worth, ROI, and payback period does not require math skills beyond addition, subtraction, multiplication, and division. Review all the examples and cases and you'll notice this. You can definitely do it!

3. To calculate worth and ROI, it is necessary to state performance outcomes in economic terms—hard numbers. Yes. However, there are ways to convert less tangible outcomes to numbers. The resources at the back of this book can help.

4. It is best to begin your calculating-worth and ROI adventures with relatively easy cases. Don't look for trouble at the outset. Start with very tangible projects. Once you have had success with these, stretch.

5. Worth is a benefit-to-cost ratio. Enough said.

6. ROI says here's how much money you will make as a percentage once you recoup your original investment. This is why you subtract cost from value before dividing by cost and multiplying by 100 to obtain a percent.

7. When calculating internal people's fully loaded costs, you multiply the base salary by three. This accounts for the full range of overhead costs. While the fully loaded cost factor varies, in general, three is a usual number found in the literature. "Semiloaded" includes only salary plus benefits and sick leave, which runs about 1.5. Always verify with your finance or human resources department to obtain the appropriate factor you should use.

8. The revenues or profits your organization does not earn because a person is in training and not doing his or her job is called lost opportunity cost. It is the opportunity the organization loses to earn money via the worker.

9. In calculating value, it is essential to work with your client's team to estimate individual improvement values, frequencies, and percentage of impact on performance. If you use numbers generated with the help of your client/client's experts, your business case will be more credible.

10. When estimating value, establish a lowest to highest range. Averages can be meaningless if there are large spreads. Ranges communicate more powerfully.

What a wonderful trip you have taken since the first chapter of this book. You now have so many of the essential tools to transform yourself from training order-taker to performance consultant. Just a few things left for you to do—some mental sorting. For this, we have prepared a fun chapter that brings us back to the start of *Training Ain't Performance*.

Chapter 11

Hit or Myth: Separating Fact From Workplace Performance Fiction

Chapter Highlights:

◆ Hit-or-Myth game that separates workplace performance fact from fiction
◆ Research-based debriefing
◆ Practical advice: remain vigilant in the face of tradition

During and immediately following World War II, there was a marked interest in propaganda and its impact on people. Numerous studies delved into how propaganda was received and perceived. Of particular interest was whether people retained and "believed" what they heard. One interesting and frequently replicated finding had to do with credibility of source. In various experiments, subjects were randomly assigned to different groups and given identical information. However, what varied was to whom the information was attributed: a high credibility source such as Winston Churchill or a low one such as Joseph Goebbels, Hitler's chief propagandist.

In immediate post-tests, subjects recalled information attributed to high credibility sources more readily than what had been attributed to the low credibility sources and expressed belief in what they recalled. Interestingly, however, six weeks to two months later, recall of information was about equal. The recall level of subjects in the high-credibility-of-source groups significantly declined while the low-credibility-of-source groups' recall levels considerably rose. Figure 11-1 illustrates the recall findings. Subjects also tended to perceive what they had retained as "fact."

While about the same amount of information was retained over time in both groups, most subjects forgot who the source of the information had been and tended to believe what they had retained. Conclusion: Propaganda can be effective!

In the same vein, many of us remember information we obtained somewhere. When we repeat or hear it repeated frequently enough, we end up believing it. Examples of this are:

- Opals bring bad luck.
- The French are arrogant (or great lovers).
- Irradiated food is dangerous to your health.
- Sweeteners turn to formaldehyde in the body and can poison you.

(Please don't remember these.)

The consequences of retaining inaccurate pieces of information (stereotypes are an excellent example) can be damaging—even devastating—depending on how pernicious and widespread they are.

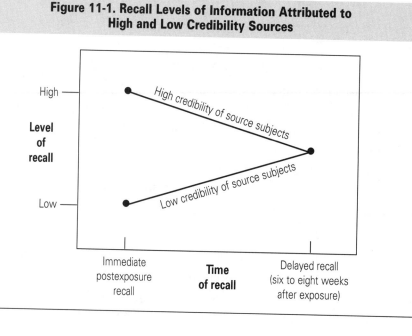

Figure 11-1. Recall Levels of Information Attributed to High and Low Credibility Sources

In the world of workplace performance, it is amazing to hear how many myths are bandied about as if they were irrefutable truths. The results in these instances can lead us down false paths, toward wasted expenditures and loss of credibility with those whom we most seek to help improve performance.

How do you arm yourself to avoid perpetuating pseudoscientific beliefs or acting on baseless enthusiasms? As important, how do you prepare yourself to do battle with those who argue strongly for what are unsupported miracle interventions? One way is to question these seemingly reasonable ideas rationally and obtain factual material that allows us to assess their credibility.

To help you do this, we have created a Hit-or-Myth game for you to play that includes a dozen statements related to workplace performance. Examine each of these in Table 11-1 and decide whether or not you believe it to be true—a hit—or false—a myth. Go with your "gut feelings." It's a game so don't try to outfox or out-guess us. The purpose of this activity is for you to make a judgment about some commonly accepted beliefs and then receive factual information that will enhance your performance consulting skills and knowledge base when encountering these beliefs in your work environment. Once you're done, we'll debrief your game choices together. Ready for the challenge? Go . . .

Have you made all your choices? Doing so will increase the meaningfulness of the activity for you as we debrief each statement. It should also result in increased retention.

Feedback on Your Hit-or-Myth Adventures

1. To achieve higher overall worker performance, hire for job-specific competencies rather than characteristics.

There is no doubt that people you hire must possess basic technical competencies and suitable experience to survive and function within a job. However, the notion that the most competent will necessarily perform the best is not necessarily true. Chalk statement number one up as a myth. Just ask successful companies such as Southwest Airlines, the most profitable North American airline company for many years. From the hundreds of thousands of applications it receives annually, it selects very few. Singapore Airlines, another greatly admired (and profitable) airline, follows a similar pattern. Both focus more on characteristics than technical skills (although they do not ignore these, obviously). These companies and others (e.g., Enterprise Rent-a-Car, the largest North American car rental company; PeopleSoft; Subaru-Isuzu) do not seek out the brightest, competency-wise. They focus very

Table 11-1. Performance Hit-or-Myth Game

Statement	Hit	Myth
1. To achieve higher overall worker performance, hire for job-specific competencies rather than characteristics.	☐	☐
2. Increases in job satisfaction tend to result in improved worker performance.	☐	☐
3. On average, high performers are about 30 percent more productive than average performers.	☐	☐
4. Personality-type inventories used for selection purposes are strong predictors of job performance success.	☐	☐
5. When people select work goals on their own, their motivation to achieve them is greater.	☐	☐
6. In the early stages of learning to solve problems, extensive practice in problem solving is more effective than studying worked-out solutions to problems.	☐	☐
7. Pay for performance is a fair way of rewarding superior performance.	☐	☐
8. Organized, supervised work teams tend to outperform self-managed teams.	☐	☐
9. Immediate feedback for improving performance on complex tasks is more effective than delayed feedback.	☐	☐
10. We are pretty accurate judges of our own specific knowledge and performance capabilities.	☐	☐
11. Executives who clearly recognize the importance of investment in their employees tend to spend more on developing employee performance capabilities and measuring results.	☐	☐
12. As more companies have become concerned about the return on their learning and performance improvement investments, activities to measure ROI have increased significantly.	☐	☐

strongly on cultural fit, ability to work in teams, service orientation, and other critical characteristics.

The most competent do not necessarily translate into the best performing. Often, they move on more rapidly to "greener grass" opportunities. There are research studies demonstrating that cultural fit and compatibility with an organization's values are strong predictors of work performance and retention—stronger than job-specific (i.e., technical) competencies. Several worthwhile reading references on this issue are listed in the For Further Reading section at the back of this book.

2. Increases in job satisfaction tend to result in improved worker performance.

This appears to be so intuitively logical that you would certainly be tempted to call this a hit. However, what appears logical may not necessarily be correct. Rate this as one of those enticing myths. This is important because a belief that happy workers are the key ingredient to workplace success can easily lead you into making performance intervention choices that will not produce desired results. Let's dig a bit deeper. Our comments on this and all the other hit-or-myth statements are based on research studies listed in the For Further Reading section. One significant meta-analytic study by Fried (1991) examined much of the extant research literature on work satisfaction and performance. What Fried found was "dissimilarity . . . in relationships of . . . performance and . . . satisfaction . . . particularly substantial" (page 690). Another major study on personnel in the high-technology industry concluded that job satisfaction and performance are not significantly correlated. One of our favorite quotes comes from a comprehensive experimental study by two researchers, Iaffaldana and Muchinsky (1985). They found that the satisfaction-performance relation constitutes an "illusory correlation."

Research on the relationship between job satisfaction and workplace performance has turned up other interesting findings, such as that information on job satisfaction can bias performance appraisals. Supervisors who randomly received information on how performers feel about their jobs, for example, tended to rate the performance of those they were told "liked their jobs" more highly than those for whom they had no information about job satisfaction. They also rated even lower the job performance of those whom they were told were dissatisfied.

A last point about this myth. In your performance consulting role, you have to be able to not only counter myths but also offer effective alternatives. Lee, a well-known researcher in this area, found three useful keys for improving performance through his study of young engineers (1992). Rather than focus on job satisfaction, he discovered that effective management of work patterns, encouragement, and support of more intensive work effort and job challenge result in significantly improved performance. What a powerful message for those seeking to influence practices that lead to desired performance outcomes!

3. On average, high performers are about 30 percent more productive than average performers.

This statement may be somewhat unfair. Yes, it is true that high performers outperform the average types by quite a bit. What's wrong with the statement and what makes it a myth is that it does not go far enough. Several respectable studies suggest that the differences range between 40 and 67 percent. Imagine the impact on your organization if you could help increase average performance to approach such exemplary levels. Thomas Gilbert (1996), in his book *Human Competence: Engineering Worthy Performance,* writes about the potential for improved performance, or the PIP. He defines PIP as the ratio of exemplary worker's output to that of the average worker: PIP = W_{ex}/W_{av}. If your exemplary workers produce $2,000 in profits and your average workers $1,000, the PIP = 2,000/1,000 or 2:1.

There is strong evidence that by identifying the key differences in exemplary and average performance and creating effective performance interventions and management systems that support exemplary behaviors and accomplishments, organizations can achieve remarkable gains. Most of the interventions have little to do with training, although where skills and knowledge are inadequate, training can definitely help. Adopting effective recruitment and selection practices; creating clear expectations and feedback mechanisms; providing appropriate work procedures, tools, and resources; and applying adequate performance management practices perceived as fair and equitable can all trigger increased desired performance. Know that the PIP in most organizations far exceeds 30 percent. Apply your performance consulting knowledge to achieve substantial gains.

4. Personality-type inventories used for selection purposes are strong predictors of job performance success.

Not according to much of the respectable scientific research evidence. Myth. Now for a bit of elaboration. When it comes to selection (and often promotion), the main use of type indicators and other similar instruments seems to be one of matching people's personalities or trait types to the job. The key problem is that research findings suggest that many of these tests, some given to millions of individuals annually, do not measure the same categories of traits (personality types) in the same manner every time. People taking the same tests at different times often achieve markedly different scores. Several studies, including two conducted by highly respected research institutions and researchers on a very widely used trait type test, concluded that the validity of this test had not been clearly established, going even further to suggest lack of evidence that identification of a person's trait type was a reliable or valid predictor of future behaviors and, presumably, performance. A National Research Council study found that 60 to 88 percent of subjects in a controlled study changed their type of classification in a five-week time period.

The popularity of and belief in these types of tests persist. As an emerging performance consultant, it is valuable for you to be aware that the results of these instruments are suspect. View the results of such tools with a healthy dose of skepticism. Rely more on performance-based testing, observation, and a broad array of indicators in guiding your judgments about selection.

5. When people select work goals on their own, their motivation to achieve them is greater.

Myth. Disappointing, isn't it? In the age of worker empowerment, many believe that people must select work goals on their own for these to be meaningful and motivating for them. Research evidence does not support this apparently reasonable assumption. People are readily willing to accept and buy into assigned work goals if—and here is where the performance consultant plays a powerful role—certain conditions are met: Those who set the goals are perceived as trustworthy and credible; the goal is presented in a personally meaningful way that inspires belief and confidence; the goal applies to all evenly and fairly, and is a call to everyone to achieve outstanding results; achievement of the goal allows (even encourages and supports) individuals and teams to select the appropriate means for them to achieve it; and in the communication of the goal is a clear expression that those who are responsible for achieving it are up to the challenge.

This all suggests that as a performance consultant, your role is not necessarily to get people to set goals, but rather to help organizational leadership articulate goals appropriately and to help set the conditions for goal achievement success.

6. In the early stages of learning to solve problems, extensive practice in problem solving is more effective than studying worked-out solutions to problems.

You want to develop problem solvers. Then it seems evident that you should put them to work solving problems right from the get-go. "Seems evident" are the key words. Another myth. A great deal of recent research evidence supports the study of problems already worked out as both a more efficient and effective way of increasing problem-solving performance. In *Telling Ain't Training*, we described how people learn and how they process information. New learning soon overloads our short-term memory's capacity to handle information. Frequent practice can rapidly multiply the amount of information the learner has to hold on to. Learning efficiency declines. Worked-out problems, presented in a structured manner, can relieve some of the short-term memory burden. Result: The focus is on the most elegant set of problem-solution steps and a higher probability of comprehension and retention.

The research in this area has led to the conclusion that the study and use of worked-out sample problems decreases learning effort and promotes more efficient transfer to new problem situations. This is useful information in guiding your decisions to develop problem-solving performance. However, a note of caution. This appears to work with more novice problem solvers. Once they have acquired strong capability in a given problem-solving area, practice becomes more effective than continuing to study worked-out solutions.

> 7. Pay for performance is a fair way of rewarding superior performance.

You do a better job than others. You achieve better results. You should be more highly rewarded. Sounds good. Despite the apparent reasonableness of this statement, it is a myth.

There are many dimensions to this issue. First, we have to make a distinction between pay for superior performance and piecework. In the latter case, pay is given for each piece produced, either in the form of so much a piece (e.g., dress sewn, bird house produced, telephone interview completed) or as a commission on a sale. Theoretically, there is no limit to what can be earned. In the case of pay for performance, or merit pay, a number of problems arise. We could cover many pages filled with documented evidence on these. We summarize the key ones here:

- Pay for performance is often administered within various salary ranges based on a fixed pool of money determined centrally. The result is that a person who performs in exemplary fashion initially receives large rewards (raises, bonuses). Eventually, she or he approaches a ceiling beyond which pay based on performance evaporates.
- In most modern work environments, people work interdependently. Identifying who did what with what result has become increasingly difficult. Perceived fairness becomes an issue. As Herbert Simon, Nobel-winning economist, has stated: ". . . the greater the interdependence among various members of an organization, the more difficult it is to measure their separate contributions" (1991).
- Perceptions of performance rather than objective measures often enter into the equation. Bias and subjectivity can influence rewards. For example, studies have found that those who hired or promoted an individual tended to rate his or her performance more highly than those who were not involved in the selection.
- Rewarding individuals, sometimes perceived as at the team's expense, can result in resentment and a decrease in overall performance.
- Individuals rewarded for their performance are encouraged to focus on themselves and not necessarily on the organization's performance.
- Pay for performance generally encourages focus on short-term results rather than long-term strategies.

To sum up, pay for performance schemes are so fraught with flaws and obstacles that, as William Mercer (1997) in discussing pay for performance points out, "Most plans share two attributes: they absorb vast amounts of management time and resources, and they make everybody unhappy" (page 61).

8. Organized, supervised work teams tend to outperform self-managed teams.

This statement is an easy one to handle. It is definitely a myth. Despite a great deal of rhetoric, many organizations maintain lingering, nostalgic sentiment for command and control practices. The bottom line, however, is that more than 20 years of research on self-managed versus closely controlled and supervised work teams overwhelmingly support self-management. These teams significantly outperform the traditionally supervised teams in most empirical studies.

The advantages are:

- Workers control themselves, thus decreasing the time and resources required for management to do this. Benefits include closer work coordination, less slacking off, and reductions in absenteeism in addition to improved productivity.
- Workers share ideas and solutions to problems that they experience and can immediately implement the remedies. The benefits are shared ownership of work problems, solutions, and results.
- Collaboration and self-direction of work teams reduce levels of supervision, administrative tracking of people's tasks and performance, and elimination of excess, unproductive personnel. The benefits are more rapid execution of decisions and decrease in overhead costs.

Other benefits such as increased loyalty, mutual support, and identification of creative and innovative ways to perform jobs also occur under the self-management umbrella. Frequently, the team finds ways to improve individual team-member performance or bring new hires up to speed without turning to formal training. All of this offers considerable, tantalizing grist for your performance improvement mill.

9. Immediate feedback for improving performance on complex tasks is more effective than delayed feedback.

Intuitively what would you prefer if you had just performed a difficult, complicated task—immediate feedback on how you had performed or feedback received hours or even a day or two later? Virtually everyone to whom we pose this question opts for immediate. Nevertheless, with respect to effectiveness in improving performance, the statement is a myth. Numerous studies comparing the effects of immediate and delayed feedback tend to arrive at the same general conclusions. Immediate feedback appears to work well with simple and/or familiar tasks. With complex tasks, many studies suggest use of delayed feedback varying from hours to days.

One major explanation for the value of delayed feedback turns once again to the constraints of our short-term memory, especially our working memory. With complex tasks, the working memory soon becomes overloaded. Details linger when immediate feedback is given, thus overburdening the working memory capacity and decreasing comprehension, retention, and recall. A delay allows time for the brain to process what has been done. Working memory is less filled with detail when feedback occurs. In some instances, feedback has been shown to be most effective just prior to another task attempt as opposed to immediately following one.

For performance consultants, feedback is an important issue. It is often cited as one of the most powerful means for improving performance. This is only true if administered appropriately. Focused on task and not on the person, provided at the correct moment, and presented in the correct manner, feedback acts as a key intervention in your performance consulting repertoire.

> 10. We are pretty accurate judges of our own specific knowledge and performance capabilities.

Who knows us better than we ourselves? Surely, we have a strong sense of what we know about specific topics and how well we can perform most things. Right? Sorry. Myth. True, in a general way, we know what we know and can or can't do. Examples of this are:

- I can't fly an airplane.
- I can speak French.
- I know European geography pretty well.
- I can't do swan dives.

When it comes to very specific skills and knowledge required by our jobs, the relationship between what we think we know and can do and actual capability drops like a stone. Examples of this are:

- I know how to overcome an angry objection during a sale.
- I can't convert a service call to a sale.
- I can't solve story problems in math.
- I know all the key points of comparison between our product line and our competitors.

A significant body of research demonstrates experimentally the poor "calibration" (the technical term used for the correlation between the confidence rating about one's specific skills and knowledge and actual performance) in judging ourselves. This even extends to judgments about how much learners think they learned from instruction and how much they actually did learn as demonstrated in post-test performance.

Want to go even further? How about gaining performance capability from what we prefer compared to arbitrarily or randomly selected methods? Wouldn't you guess that we acquire skills and knowledge better from preferred approaches? By now, you no longer trust us—and rightly so. The research (and again we encourage you to turn to the For Further Reading section of this volume) suggests that regardless of preference, methods that include significant amounts of relevant practice with appropriate feedback lead to improved performance results.

Bottom line? Take care lest you be overly swayed by what performers say they know and can do or express preferences for a particular mode of intervention. Verify by performance testing or through performance data gathering. Apply principles from learning and performance research to select and develop your interventions.

> 11. Executives who clearly recognize the importance of investment in their employees tend to spend more on developing employee performance capabilities and measuring results.

According to an in-depth survey of 250 executives (including CEOs) across a broad range of companies and industries, this is not the case. Alas, another myth! Although 85 percent of the executives surveyed stated that they recognized the critical importance of investment in tangible assets such as their employees, less than 35 percent admitted that they, in fact, put their money where their convictions lay. The CEOs in the survey ranked employee retention as one of the top two measurements of value creation for their companies, but did not include this in their formal reporting structures, did not carefully measure the factors affecting this, and cited current costs and unsatisfactory measurement systems as reasons for not doing more.

> 12. As more companies have become concerned about the return on their learning and performance improvement investments, activities to measure ROI have increased.

We won't tease you with this one. Sad to say, this is a myth. It also presents a strange paradox. In the ASTD 2002 *State of the Industry* report on trends in employer-provided training (and by extension, associated performance improvement activities), of the top ten, here is the number one trend "affecting workplace learning and performance" (page 4):

> "1. Money: Increasing pressure from shareholders for short-term profits means that there is greater pressure on employees to produce results and on training to show a return on investment."

Get the message? The pressure is on for ROI evaluations. And the response? In self-reports (which tend to inflate practices seen as positive), training investment leaders—those that spend the most per employee—state that they evaluate results (a.k.a., Kirkpatrick's level 4 evaluation) only 7 percent of the time. With respect to evaluating return on expectations, their activities drop to 4 percent. What is even more disheartening is that this is a decline from the previous year (results: 11 percent versus 7 percent; return on expectations: 5 percent versus 4 percent). The report summarizes the situation in this way (page 24):

> "A number of stakeholder groups identified increasing pressure to demonstrate the return from training (and other performance improvement activities) as a key trend. It is somewhat troubling that in general, firms did not appear to be increasing their efforts to evaluate the impact of the training they provide."

Somewhat troubling? We suggest that it is very scary. As we pointed out in chapter 10, it is essential that you demonstrate in business terms what you contribute to your organization. You've got the message. Training ain't performance. It takes a whole lot more to achieve valued behaviors and accomplishments. When we achieve these, it is crucial that we communicate our successes in a credible manner.

Was the hit-or-myth activity worthwhile for you? Enlightening? Even fun? True, we set you up by making every statement a myth, but our purpose was honorable: to prepare you to do battle against the forces of those who would impose interventions based on false or shaky foundations.

The Bottom Line on Performance

Our mission—and now yours, we hope—as performance consultants who care about helping organizations attain valued accomplishments through people requires that we apply principles and make decisions based on the most valid evidence available. There are many more myths surrounding us with respect to performance such as:

◆ Discovery and exploratory strategies for improving learning and performance are more effective than directive ones (only true in certain instances).

◆ Competency-based systems ensure job success.

◆ Most organizational change initiatives result in performance improvement benefits.

◆ Technology investments are the main causal factor in recent increased productivity.

Each of these must be challenged. Accepting them without first examining the data can easily result in wasted effort and negative consequences to our organizations and to us professionally. The key to making the right intervention decisions is in being cause-conscious, not solution-focused and in getting the facts rather than accepting commonly held myths about the workplace and people performance. That's the bottom line.

A Final Hit-or-Myth Frolic: Match Your Wits to Ours

Here's a final exercise to prepare you for the "myth-taken" notions you may face in the workplace. In the second column of the exercise, we have randomly placed our dozen myth-conceptions quoted by a fellow worker, client, even another performance consultant. The next column provides you with a list of counter arguments, identified by a capital letter, and in no particular order. Your task is to match the correct argument to each myth-leading statement, and put your answer in the box on the left. Go for it!

Worksheet 11-1. They Say . . . You Say . . .

Your match	They say . . .	You counter with . . .
☐	1. Include immediate feedback. It always works better than delayed feedback, especially on these complex tasks they have to perform.	A. Research evidence shows that what executives believe about the importance of their employees and investing in their development does not necessarily translate into dollars. Of 250 executives surveyed, 85 percent expressed conviction of the importance in investing in employees, but only 35 percent said they paid up.
☐	2. If these new hires are going to have to solve problems, give them lots of problem-solving practice right from the start.	B. These types of tests may be used by millions, but scientific research casts doubt on their validity as a predictor of performance success. A National Research Council study found 60 to 80 percent of subjects changed type classification in a five-week period.

(continued on page 186)

Worksheet 11-1. They Say . . . You Say . . . (continued)

Your match	They say . . .	You counter with . . .
☐	3. You can probably expect our high performers to be about 20 to 30 percent more productive than our average workers.	C. Sounds fair. Experience and research show otherwise. Fixed pools of money, short-term success focus, bias in rating performance, and tendencies to pit individual performance success against team success are serious flaws in this approach. It is costly to administer, and the research suggests everyone ends up unhappy.
☐	4. Because more companies are demanding to know what they are getting from their training and performance improvement dollars, we should be finding more cases of results-oriented and ROI evaluation.	D. Unfortunately, it's not the case. Only 7 percent of the training investment leaders evaluated results and 4 percent return on expectations in 2002. This was a significant decline from the previous year.
☐	5. Let our people select their own work goals. They will certainly be more motivated to achieve them than if our leadership sets the goals.	E. Research on problem solving with novices for a particular subject or work situation strongly favors studying worked-out problems initially. It reduces cognitive load and produces superior problem-solving results.
☐	6. I'd suggest a popular, widely used personality trait instrument to select the right candidate. It should help predict job performance success.	F. Self-motivated teams control themselves, thus reducing management time and resources. They share better; take ownership of the work and results; become more loyal; bring in new workers more easily; and, best of all, perform better.
☐	7. Set up organized, supervised work teams. They are bound to outperform self-managed teams.	G. Research doesn't support the belief that self-selected work goals result in greater motivation to achieve them. If the workers trust the leaders who set the goals; find the goals fair, appropriate, and achievable; and sense the leaders have confidence in people's ability to attain success, they are just as, and sometimes even more, motivated than if they set goals themselves.

Your match	They say . . .	You counter with . . .
☐	8. Seek out those with the highest competency ratings as your major criterion for selection. You'll get the best performance from them.	H. Many studies demonstrate that we don't always know what we think we know or believe we can do, and vice versa. The correlation between confidence in our knowledge and performance capability and actual results is called calibration. In many studies, the correlation is zero.
☐	9. Our executives believe in the importance of investing in our people. We can therefore expect more money for developing their performance capabilities.	I. Research suggests that while immediate feedback is effective for simple tasks, delayed feedback appears to be more effective for complex tasks. The reason: Working memory is often overloaded just after completing a complex task. It has to free itself of the details to comprehend and treat new feedback information.
☐	10. Focus on building job satisfaction. You'll get better performance.	J. The relationship between job satisfaction and performance is as one study puts it "illusory." What seems more important is effective management of work patterns, encouragement, support of more intensive work effort, and job challenge.
☐	11. If you want superior performance, set up a merit pay system that pays for improved performance results.	K. Too conservative. Research shows the percentages to be higher—40 to 67 percent. Measure the difference between exemplary and average performance (the PIP—potential for improved performance). Work to bring average performers up to exemplary levels.
☐	12. I asked our people about what they know and can do with respect to this project. Let's work from the data I collected.	L. While competency is important, research suggests that characteristics are better predictors of performance and retention. Hire for characteristics (and adequate skills and knowledge). Train and develop for competencies.

Here are the matches:

1 – I	2 – E	3 – K	4 – D	5 – G	6 – B
7 – F	8 – L	9 – A	10 – J	11 – C	12 – H

How well did you do? If you matched 10 or more correctly, bravo. You are well armed to make solid performance decisions about performance improvement. Less than 10, we suggest you review the hit-or-myth exercise to improve your competence and confidence in this area. You will find the value of separating beliefs and enthusiasms from respectably verified findings to be a tremendous asset to your professional efforts in improving performance.

This chapter is done. But we're not quite ready to part from you. Please hang in with us for a few more short pages. We'd like to close out our dialogue with you by presenting a few concluding reflections. Then we'll say adieu, but not goodbye. We'd love to continue sharing ideas with you. We'll let you know how you can do this in the final chapter.

Chapter 12

The Finale but Not the End

Chapter Highlights:

◆ Summary of the book's contents
◆ Review of key messages
◆ Parting reflection on values

This concluding chapter has four major purposes. The first is to review the trip we have taken together and emphasize key points to retain as you part company from *Training Ain't Performance*. The second is to summarize the main messages we have shared with you. Third, we'd like to leave you with some thoughts concerning the values that should guide the performance consultant—ones we, ourselves, have taken to heart and apply daily in our professional work and conduct. Finally, we don't want this conversation to end so we will provide you with opportunities for maintaining a conversation with us after you have put this book away.

A Rapid Review of *Training Ain't Performance*

Remember way back in chapter 1 when we began with Melvyn and Marna, our ambitious bankers? This is where we started our exploration of what "performance" is and shared with you the theme and purpose of this book. We promised an interactive, application-focused, friendly, easy-to-read style and have worked hard to keep our word.

Chapter 2 dealt with key vocabulary terms, some from our previous companion volume, *Telling Ain't Training*, such as *training, instruction, education,* and *learning*.

Others, specific to this one, included *behavior, accomplishment, performance, worth,* and *value*. We said you would encounter these repeatedly in the succeeding chapters and so you have. In this same chapter you also discovered the performance improvement mantra. Remember it? "Cause-conscious not solution-focused." You came away from chapter 2 with an effective sentence to set your clients at ease while not promising training, but reassuring them that you would help in achieving the results they desire: "I can help you solve your problem." The chapter closed with a discussion on where technology fits—as appropriate—and an overview of the remaining chapters.

In chapter 3, you worked on the case of ProtoPlasmics Biotech where you discovered that a request for training, when carefully probed, can lead to other more relevant interventions. This fed into the organizational human performance system model and the case of Harry's Diner. One conclusion from this chapter was that it is possible to engineer performance systems in ways all stakeholders value.

"What is my greatest performance block?" That was the opener from chapter 4. This led to discovering the importance of environmental factors affecting performance and the Thomas Gilbert Behavior Engineering Model. Applying this model to the Harry's Diner case demonstrated its usefulness. The chapter concluded with three forces that must be aligned to achieve performance success: work, workplace, and worker.

Then it was on to lengthy chapter 5, Engineering Effective Performance. Here, step by step and with examples, you acquired an operational-procedural model for attaining desired performance. As you walked through each of the 10 steps, you applied them to cases and collected a number of useful tools. In many ways, this chapter constituted the heart of *Training Ain't Performance*. It is here that you acquired a detailed model and means for becoming a performance consultant.

Chapter 6 took over where the previous chapter left off. It presented you with your new mission as a performance consultant, described new roles, and guided your thinking to help you transform from training order-taker to performance consultant.

Chapter 7 returned to training—maybe necessary in circumstances where there are skill and knowledge gaps, but rarely sufficient. Here you received a shortcut approach to identifying when training isn't the answer. This included watching out for key words and phrases that should twitch your antennae. The chapter also cautioned that there are times training groups have a vested interest *not* to improve performance, thus creating a never-ending market for their programs. Transfer of training-learning to the workplace was also examined along with how to increase its probability of occurring—by helping supervisors prepare trainees beforehand and supporting them post-training.

In chapter 8 you were provided with an extensive menu of interventions of both the learning and nonlearning variety. Worksheets laid out the many options at your disposal, described and explained each of these, offered sample applications, and then encouraged you to select and/or create your own interventions relevant to your work setting. With all this in hand, you were prepared for the next challenge.

Chapter 9 confirmed that you were well along the performance consulting path and ready to make it happen. After defining *performance, consulting,* and *performance consultant,* you moved on to the competencies you require to fulfill your mission of improving human performance. The chapter also dealt with important personal characteristics you require to be effective. It stressed the importance of building credibility and trust, partnerships, and your own expertise. It concluded with a wise reminder that we do not own the performance problems and their solutions. The clients have overall responsibility for these. We can assist in helping them meet their responsibilities through actions, which were detailed in chapter 9.

Chapter 10 stood somewhat alone, yet not completely. Its theme, The Bottom Line, is critical in today's competitive environment. In this chapter, you acquired tools and skills for calculating worth, return-on-investment, and payback period. This places you well ahead of many others.

Finally, chapter 11 confronted you with a dozen hit-or-myth statements, had you decide the truth of each one, and then presented you with research-based information. Its purpose was to prepare you for meeting the many enthusiasms and beliefs you will encounter out there on the performance battlefield. Forewarned is forearmed.

 So now we have arrived at the end of our voyage. What are the most important take-aways—the key messages? In brief:

- First and foremost, training ain't performance. Don't let training become the default intervention for improving performance in your environment.
- Rarely, if ever, do single solutions work with complex performance problems.
- Start with the environmental factors before you turn to "fixing" the performers.
- Show key stakeholders the money. Talk business not training. Demonstrate the worth and ROI of your contributions.
- Don't let anyone overwhelm you with the latest and greatest enthusiasms or old truisms. Separate myth from fact. Let science and respectable information-gathering be your guides for improving performance.

In summary, not only is it true that training ain't performance, nothing else is either except for the valued accomplishments and appropriate behaviors we help people in our organizations achieve. If you've understood this, then we have accomplished the mission of this book.

Some Parting Reflections—On Values

The work we do is more than a job or even a profession. It is a passion. We believe that there is no greater gift we can offer to our fellow workers than the ability to achieve successes that they value. Despite cynical rhetoric, most people want to do well in their work. We can help them solve their problems and, in doing so, bring about valued accomplishments for their organizations, shareholders, and the community at large. This is how we have chosen to contribute and, obviously, what we hope you, too, will wish to do.

 This leads us to share our performance consulting values with you. These are what guide us in every aspect of our professional lives. We offer them as a starting point for your own reflections.

- Our clients are, or become, professional friends. They are as delighted to work with us as we are with them.
- We are fully committed to our clients' best interests. We address their needs with the most cost-effective solutions.
- We provide greater value than our cost.
- We perform our services in partnership with our clients in a nonthreatening manner.
- We apply only the highest standards of ethical and professional conduct in our work.
- Our professional practice is based upon the scientific principles of human performance technology and its respected precedents.
- We develop and support our associates and colleagues in their personal and professional growth.
- Our aim is to build maximum client self-sufficiency, not consultant dependency.
- We encourage and support our clients in their own professional growth.
- We accept responsibility. We allow ourselves to accept congratulations for our successes, because we are prepared to live with the consequences of our failures.
- We welcome challenges that allow us to stretch and expand our competencies.
- We treat commitments, promises, and professional relationships as sacred trusts.

A professional practice without a set of values to guide your choices and conduct can be dangerous. As you have seen from the outset of this volume, our focus has been on performance—the valued accomplishments of behaviors. In this, values play a vital role.

Only Adieu and Not Goodbye

The preceding values also appear on our Website at www.hsa-lps.com. We encourage you to come visit us there as well as at professional conferences sponsored by ASTD, ISPI, *Training Magazine*/VNU Learning, and others because we're often there. Our Website contains publications and tools you can download free of charge. You can ask questions and contact us to chat. Although this book has ended, the conversation has only begun . . . .

For Further Reading

Achieving desired workplace performance from people requires a highly systematic approach to the analysis of performance gaps and a broad knowledge of the range of potential interventions to eliminate them. *Training Ain't Performance* has introduced you to the basic concepts and models and provided you with a solid foundation to begin your performance consulting work. Now, as you set out on your journey of helping to close performance gaps, you will find that you require more knowledge and tools to support your professional efforts.

This section provides you with a wonderfully exciting, broad spectrum of reading resources. We drew from many of these ourselves as we developed this book. What we list, chapter by chapter, either substantiates our assertions; offers additional depth, examples, and insights to help strengthen your understanding of the various themes; or advances beyond what we have presented and breaks new ground.

Before delving into these resources, here are a few explanatory notes. First, you will see references to human performance technology, or HPT. This is a field of study and professional practice that underlies and supports performance consulting and the systematic efforts to improve human performance. Many universities offer graduate programs in HPT. We encourage you to explore the HPT writings. Second, as you will soon notice, most of the resources listed are of a professional nature. Unlike *Telling Ain't Training*, where we cited many research studies on human learning, we felt that the performance consulting field, which is about engineering interventions based on practical considerations, lent itself more to the writings of professional practitioners. However, we selected carefully those that we believe possess solid, respectable bases for their published works. Finally, the array of proposed resources may appear daunting. Be at ease. Like items in an extensive menu, they are there to whet your appetite. Select only what tempts your palate and you can readily digest. Nourish yourself over time. We promise that what we offer here will help you in developing as a mature performance improvement professional.

Chapter 2: What's in a Word?

Baldwin, T.T., and Ford, J.K. (1988). Transfer of training: a review and directions for future research. *Personnel psychology, 41* (1), 63-105.

Broad, M.L., and Newstrom, J.W. (1992). *Transfer of training: action-packed strategies to ensure high payoff from training investments.* Reading, MA: Addison-Wesley.

Ford, J.K., and Weissbein, D.A. (1997). Transfer of training: an updated review and analysis. *Performance improvement quarterly, 10* (2), 22-41.

Fuller, J., and Farrington, J. (1998). *From training to performance improvement: navigating the transition.* Washington, DC: International Society for Performance Improvement/Amherst, MA: HRD Press, Inc.

Gilbert, T.F. (1996). *Human competence: engineering worthy performance.* Washington, DC: International Society for Performance Improvement/Amherst, MA: HRD Press, Inc.

Harless, J. (1970). *An ounce of analysis is worth a pound of objectives.* Newnan, GA: Harless Performance Guild.

Miles, D. (2003). *The 30-second encyclopedia of learning and performance: a trainer's guide to theory, terminology, and practice.* New York: AMACOM.

Stolovitch, H.D. (2000). *Learning and performance support best practices study: summary report.* Los Angeles: HSA Learning & Performance Solutions.

Stolovitch, H.D., and Keeps, E.J. (2002). *Telling ain't training.* Alexandria, VA: American Society for Training & Development.

———. (2002). *The HSA lexicon: over 100 definitions of human performance technology.* Los Angeles: HSA Learning & Performance Solutions. (Also available to download from http://www.hsa-lps.com/Lexicon.htm.)

Chapter 3: The Performance System

Kaufman, R.E., Oakley-Brown, H., Watkins, R., and Leigh, H. (2003). *Strategic planning for success: aligning people, performance and payoffs.* San Francisco: Jossey-Bass/Pfeiffer.

Mager, R. (1996). *What every manager should know about training: or I've got a training problem and other odd ideas.* Atlanta: The Center for Effective Performance.

Rummler, G., and Brache, A. (1995). *Improving performance: how to manage the white space on the organization chart, second edition.* San Francisco: Jossey-Bass.

Stolovitch, H.D., and Keeps, E.J. (1999). What is human performance technology? In H.D. Stolovitch and E.J. Keeps, editors. *Handbook of human performance technology: improving individual and organizational performance worldwide, second edition.* San Francisco: Jossey-Bass/Pfeiffer.

Chapter 4: What's My Greatest Performance Block?

Dean, P.J. (1997). Thomas F. Gilbert, PhD: Engineering performance improvement with or without training. In P.J. Dean and D.E. Ripley, editors. *Performance improvement pathfinders: models for organizational learning systems* (volume one, performance improvement series). Washington, DC: International Society for Performance Improvement.

Gilbert, T.F. (1996). *Human competence: engineering worthy performance.* Washington, DC: International Society for Performance Improvement/Amherst, MA: HRD Press, Inc.

Mager, R.F. (1997). *Analyzing performance problems.* Atlanta: The Center for Effective Performance.

Chapter 5: Engineering Effective Performance

Blanchard, K., Robinson, D., and Robinson, J. (2002). *Zap the gaps! Target higher performance and achieve it!* New York: William Morrow (an imprint of Harper Collins).

Dormant, D. (1992). Implementing human performance technology in organizations. In H.D. Stolovitch and E.J. Keeps, editors. *Handbook of human performance technology: improving individual and organizational performance worldwide.* San Francisco: Jossey-Bass/Pfeiffer.

Foshay, W.R., Silber, K.H., and Stelnicki, M. (2003). *Writing training materials that work: how to train anyone to do anything.* San Francisco: Jossey-Bass/Pfeiffer.

Harmon, P. (2002). *Business process change.* San Francisco: Morgan Kaufmann Publishers.

Kearny, L., and Smith, P. (1999). Workplace design for creative thinking. In H.D. Stolovitch and E.J. Keeps, editors. *Handbook of human performance technology: improving individual and organizational performance worldwide, second edition.* San Francisco: Jossey-Bass/Pfeiffer.

Rossett, A. (1987). *Training needs assessment.* Englewood Cliffs, NJ: Educational Technology Publications.

Russell, L. (2000). *Project management for trainers: stop "winging it" and get control of your projects.* Alexandria, VA: American Society for Training & Development.

Scheer, A.W., Abolhassan, F., Jost, W., and Kirchmer, M., editors. *Business process change management: ARIS in practice.* New York: Springer-Verlag.

Stolovitch, H.D., and Keeps, E.J. (2003). *Engineering effective learning toolkit.* San Francisco: Pfeiffer/Wiley.

———. (2004). *Front-end analysis and return on investment toolkit.* San Francisco: Pfeiffer/Wiley.

Strayer, J. (2003). *Instructional systems design revisited.* Silver Spring, MD: International Society for Performance Improvement.

Van Tiem, D., Moseley, J., and Dessinger, J.C. (2001). *Performance improvement interventions: enhancing people, processes, and organizations through performance technology.* Silver Spring, MD: International Society for Performance Improvement.

Zemke, R., and Kramlinger, T. (1982). *Figuring things out.* Reading, MA: Addison-Wesley.

Chapter 6: From Training Order-Taker to Performance Consultant

Block, P. (2000). *Flawless consulting: a guide to getting your expertise used, second edition.* San Francisco: Jossey-Bass/Pfeiffer.

Hale, J. (2003). *Performance-based management: what every manager should do to get results.* San Francisco: Pfeiffer.

Hale, J. (1998). *The performance consultant's fieldbook, includes a Microsoft Word diskette: tools and techniques for improving organizations and people.* San Francisco: Jossey-Bass/Pfeiffer.

Harless, J.H. (2000). *Analyzing human performance: tools for achieving business results.* Alexandria, VA: American Society for Training & Development.

Kinlaw, D.C. (1995). *ASTD's trainer's sourcebook: facilitation skills.* Alexandria, VA: American Society for Training & Development.

Robinson, D., and Robinson, J. (1995). *Performance consulting: moving beyond training.* San Francisco: Berrett-Koehler.

———. (1998). *Moving from training to performance: a practical guidebook.* San Francisco: Berrett-Koehler.

Chapter 7: Why Training Fails: Maybe Necessary . . . Rarely Sufficient

Arthur Jr., W.A., Bennett Jr., W., Edens, P.S., and Bell, S.T. (2003). Effectiveness of training in organizations: a meta-analysis of design and evaluation features. *Journal of applied psychology, 88* (2), 234-245.

Baldwin, T.T., and Ford, J.K. (1988). Transfer of training: a review and directions for future research. *Personnel psychology, 41,* 63-105.

British Broadcasting Corporation. (2003). Training "fails to prepare" doctors. BBC News 05/09 08:24:19 GMT. (http://news.bbc.co.uk/go/pr/fr/-1/hi/health/3010013.stm.)

Broad, M., and Newstrom, J. (1992). *Transfer of training: action-packed strategies to ensure high payoff from training investments.* Reading, MA: Addison-Wesley.

Fitzpatrick, R. (2001). The strange case of the transfer of training estimate. *The industrial-organizational psychologist, 39* (2), 18-19.

Saks, A.M. (2002). So what is a good transfer of training estimate? A reply to Fitzpatrick. *The industrial-organizational psychologist, 39* (3), 30.

Salas, E., and Cannon-Bowers, J.A. (2001). The science of training: a decade of progress. *Annual review of psychology, 52,* 471-499.

Yammill, S., and McLean, G.N. (2001). Theories supporting transfer of training. *Human resource development quarterly, 12* (2), 195-208.

Chapter 8: Panoply of Performance Interventions

Aldrich, C. (2003). *Simulations and the future of learning: an innovative (and perhaps revolutionary) approach to e-learning.* San Francisco: Jossey-Bass/Pfeiffer.

Barbazette, J. (2004). *Instant case studies: how to design, adapt and use case studies in training.* San Francisco: Pfeiffer/Wiley.

Becker, F., and Steele, F. (1994). *Workplace by design, mapping the high-performance workscape.* San Francisco: Jossey-Bass.

Brown, L. (1996). *Designing and developing electronic performance support systems.* Boston: Digital Press.

Dickelman, G.J. (2003). *EPSS revisited: a lifecycle for developing performance-centered systems.* Silver Spring, MD: International Society for Performance Improvement.

Elliott, P.H. (1999). Job aids. In H.D. Stolovitch and E.J. Keeps, editors. *Handbook of human performance technology: improving individual and organizational performance worldwide, second edition.* San Francisco: Jossey-Bass/Pfeiffer.

Harrison, N. (1998). *How to design self-directed and distance learning programs: a guide for creators of web-based training, computer-based training, and self-study materials.* New York: McGraw-Hill Trade.

Jacobs, R.L., editor. (2001). Planned training on the job. *Advances in Developing Human Resources, 3*(4). (Complete issue on structured-on-the-job training.) Thousand Oaks, CA: Sage Publications Ltd.

Kearney, L., and Smith, P. (1999). Workplace design for creative thinking. In H.D. Stolovitch and E.J. Keeps, editors. *Handbook of human performance technology: improving individual and organizational performance worldwide, second edition.* San Francisco: Jossey-Bass/Pfeiffer.

Keller, J. M. (1999). Motivational systems. In H.D. Stolovitch and E.J. Keeps, editors. *Handbook of human performance technology: improving individual and organizational performance worldwide, second edition.* San Francisco: Jossey-Bass/Pfeiffer.

Lawson, K. (1997). *Improving on-the-job training and coaching.* Alexandria, VA: American Society for Training & Development.

Leibler, S.N., and Parkman, A.W. (1999). Human resources selection. In H.D. Stolovitch and E.J. Keeps, editors. *Handbook of human performance technology: improving individual and organizational performance worldwide, second edition.* San Francisco: Jossey-Bass/Pfeiffer.

Leigh, E., and Kinder, J. (2001). *Fun and games for workplace learning.* New York: McGraw Hill.

Piskurich, G.M., Beckschi, P., and Hall, B. (1999). *The ASTD handbook of training design and delivery, second edition.* New York: McGraw-Hill Trade.

Rossett, A., and Gautier-Downes, J. (1990). *A handbook of job aids.* San Francisco: Pfeffer & Company.

Rothwell, W. J. (2000). *The intervention selector, designer and developer, and implementor.* Alexandria, VA: American Society for Training & Development.

Smith, P., and Kearny, L. (1994). *Creating workplaces where people can think.* San Francisco: Jossey-Bass.

Stolovitch, H.D., Clark, R.E., and Condley, S.J. (2002). *Incentives, motivation and workplace performance: research and best practices.* New York: SITE Foundation. (Available from www.ispi.org.)

Stolovitch, H.D., and Keeps, E.J. (1999). *Handbook of human performance technology: improving individual and organizational performance worldwide, second edition.* San Francisco: Jossey-Bass/Pfeiffer.

———. (2003). *Engineering effective learning toolkit.* San Francisco: Pfeiffer/Wiley.

Sugrue, B., and Fuller, J., editors. (1999). *Performance interventions.* Alexandria, VA: American Society for Training & Development.

Van Tiem, D.M., Moseley, J.L., and Dessinger, J.C. (2001). *Performance improvement interventions: enhancing people, processes, and organizations through performance technology.* Silver Spring, MD: International Society for Performance Improvement.

Villachica, S.W., and Stone, D.L. (1999). Performance support systems. In H.D. Stolovitch and E.J. Keeps, editors. *Handbook of human performance technology: improving individual and organizational performance worldwide, second edition.* San Francisco: Jossey-Bass/Pfeiffer.

Wolfe, J.W., and Keys, J.B. (1997). *Business simulations, games and experiential learning in business education.* Binghamton, NY: Haworth Press.

Chapter 9: Making It Happen

Esque, T., and Patterson, P. (1998). *Getting results: case studies in performance improvement.* Amherst, MA: HRD Press/Silver Spring, MD: International Society for Performance Improvement.

Robinson, D.G., and Robinson, J.C. (1995). *Performance consulting: moving beyond training.* San Francisco: Berrett-Koehler.

———. (2004). *Strategic business partner: how to get invited to the "table" and what to do when you get there!* San Francisco: Berrett-Koehler.

Rothwell, W.J. (1999). *ASTD models for human performance improvement: roles, competencies and outputs.* Alexandria, VA: American Society for Training & Development.

Stolovitch, H.D., Keeps, E.J., and Rodrigue, D. (1999). Skill sets, characteristics and values for the human performance technologist. In H.D. Stolovitch and E.J. Keeps, editors. *Handbook of human performance technology: improving individual and organizational performance worldwide, second edition.* San Francisco: Jossey-Bass/Pfeiffer.

Chapter 10: The Bottom Line: Demonstrating the Return-on-Investment of Your Performance Interventions

Friedlob, G.T., and Plewa, F.J. (1996). *Understanding return on investment.* New York: John Wiley & Sons, Inc.

Phillips, J.J. (2002). *How to measure training results.* New York: McGraw-Hill.

———. (2003). *Return on investment in training and performance improvement programs, second edition.* Burlington, MA: Butterworth-Heinemann.

Phillips, P.P. (2002). *The bottom line on ROI: basics, benefits, & barriers to measuring training & performance improvement.* Atlanta: The Center for Effective Performance.

Schneider, H., Monetta, D., and Wright, C. (1992). Training function accountability: how to really measure return on investment. *Performance & instruction, 31*(33), 12-17.

Schneider, H., and Wright, C. (1990). Return on training investment: hard measures for soft subjects. *Performance & instruction, 29* (2), 28-35.

Stolovitch, H.D, and Keeps, E.J. (2004). *Front-end analysis and return on investment toolkit.* San Francisco: Jossey-Bass/Pfeiffer.

Swanson, R., and Gradous, D. (1988). *Forecasting financial benefits of human resource development.* San Francisco: Jossey-Bass.

Yates, B.T. (1996). *Analyzing costs, procedures, processes, and outcomes in human services* (applied social research series, volume 42). Thousand Oaks, CA: Sage Publications Ltd.

Chapter 11: Hit or Myth: Separating Fact from Workplace Performance Fiction

Myth 1

Chatman, J.A. (1991). Managing people and organizations: selection and socialization in public accounting firms. *Administrative science quarterly, 36,* 459-484.

Chee, L.S. (1994). Singapore Airlines: strategic human resources initiatives. In D. Tarrington, editor. *International human resource management: think globally, act locally.* New York: Prentice-Hall.

Graham, L. (1995). *On the line at Suburu-Isuzu.* Ithaca, NY: ILR Press.

O'Reilly, B. (1996, October 28). The rent-a-car jocks who made Enterprise #1. *Fortune,* 128.

O'Reilly, C.A., Chatman, J.A., and Caldwell, D.F. (1991). People and organizational culture: a profile comparison approach to assessing person-organization fit. *Academy of management journal, 34,* 487-516.

Pfeffer, J. (1998). *The human equation: building profits by putting people first.* Boston: Harvard Business School Press, 70-74.

Myth 2

Fried, Y. (1991). Meta-analytic comparison of the job diagnostic survey and job characteristics inventory as correlates of work satisfaction and performance. *Journal of applied psychology, 76* (5), 690-698.

Iaffaldano, M., and Muchinsky, P.A. (1985). Job satisfaction and job performance: a meta-analysis. *Psychological bulletin, 97* (2), 251-273.

Lee, D.M.S. (1992). Job challenge, work effort and job performance of young engineers: a causal analysis. *IEEE transactions on engineering management, 39* (3), 214-236.

Macan, T.H. (1996). Time management training: effects on time behaviors, attitudes and job performance. *Journal of psychology, 130* (3), 229-236.

Mannheim, B., Baruch, Y., and Tal, J. (1997). Alternative models for antecedents and outcomes of work centrality and job satisfaction of high-tech personnel. *Human relations, 50* (12), 1537-1562.

Smitter, J.W., Collins, H., and Buda, R. (1989). When ratee satisfaction influences performance evaluations: a case of illusory correlation. *Journal of applied psychology, 74* (4), 599-605.

Myth 3

Axelrod, E.L., Handfield-Jones, H., and Welsh, T.A. (2001). War for talent, part two. *The McKinsey quarterly* 2. [Key points summarized in Clark, R.G., and Estes, F.E. (2002). *Turning research into results: a guide to selecting the right performance solutions.* Atlanta: The Center for Effective Performance.]

Gilbert, T.F. (1996). *Human competence: engineering worthy performance.* Washington, DC: International Society for Performance Improvement/Amherst, MA: HRD Press, Inc.

Myth 4

Druckman, D., and Bjork, R. (1991). In the mind's eye: enhancing human performance. Washington, D.C.: National Academy Press. [Key points summarized in Clark, R.G., and Estes, F.E. (2002). *Turning research into results: a guide to selecting the right performance solutions.* Atlanta: The Center for Effective Performance.]

Pittenger, D.J. (1993). Measuring the MBTI...and coming up short. *Journal of career planning and employment, 54,* 48-53.

Pittenger, D.J. (1993). The utility of the Myers-Briggs Type Indicator. *Review of educational research, 63,* 467-88.

Myth 5

Bandura, A. (1997). *Self-efficacy: the exercise of control.* New York: W.H. Freeman.

Clark, R.E. (1998). Motivating performance. *Performance improvement, 37* (8), 39-47.

Locke, E.A., and Latham, G.P. (1990). *A theory of goal setting and task performance.* Englewood Cliffs, NJ: Prentice-Hall.

Myth 6

Atkinson, R.K., Derry, S.J., Renkl, A., and Wortham, D. (2000). Learning from examples: instructional principles from the worked examples research. *Review of educational research, 70* (2), 181-214.

Clark, R.C., and Mayer, R.E. (2002). *e-Learning and the science of instruction: proven guidelines of consumers and designers of multimedia learning.* San Francisco: Jossey-Bass/Pfeiffer. (See chapter 10, pages 173-196.)

Kalyuga, S., Chandler, P., and Sweller, J. (1999). Managing split attention and redundancy in multimedia instruction. *Applied cognitive psychology, 13,* 351-372.

Paas, F.G.W.C. (1992). Training strategies for attaining transfer of problem-solving skill in statistics: a cognitive load approach. *Journal of educational psychology, 84,* 429-434.

Myth 7

Beer, M., Spector, B., Lawrence, P., Quinn Mills, D., and Walton, R. (1984). *Managing human assets.* New York: Free Press.

Hatcher, L., and Ross, J.L. (1991). From individual incentives to an organization-wide gainsharing plan: effects on teamwork and product quality. *Journal of organizational behavior, 12,* 174.

Kohn, A. (1993). *Punished by rewards.* Boston: Houghton-Mifflin.

Mercer, W. (1997, Winter). *Leader to leader, 1,* 61.

Nulty, P. (1995, November 13). Incentive pay can be crippling. *Fortune,* 235.

Pfeffer, J. (1998). *The human equation: building profits by putting people first.* Boston: Harvard Business School Press, 203-213.

Schoarman, F.D. (1988). Escalation bias in performance appraisals: an unintended consequence of supervisor participation in hiring decisions. *Journal of applied psychology, 73,* 58-62.

Simon, H.A. (1991). Organization and markets. *Journal of economic perspectives, 5,* 33.

Storey, J., and Sisson, K. (1993). *Managing human resources and industrial relations.* Buckingham, UK: Open University Press.

Wood, S. (1996). High commitment management and payment systems. *Journal of management studies, 33,* 55.

Myth 8

Banker, R.D., Field, J.M., Schroeder, R.G., and Sinha, K.K. (1996). Impact of work teams on manufacturing performance: a longitudinal field study. *Academy of management journal, 39,* 867-890.

Batt, R. (1996). Outcomes of self-directed workgroups in telecommunications services. In P.B. Voss, editor. *Proceedings of the forty-eighth annual meeting of the industrial relations research association.* Madison, WI: Industrial Relations Research Association.

Fishman, C. (1996, April-May). Whole Foods teams. *Fast Company,* 104.

Graham, L. (1995). *On the line at Suburu-Isuzu.* Ithaca, NY: ILR Press.

Shaiken, H., Lopez, S., and Mankita, I. (1996, January). Two routes to team production: Saturn and Chrysler compared. *Industrial relations, 36,* 31.

Whole Foods Market. (1995). Annual Report. Austin, TX.

Myth 9

Clariana, R.B. (1999). Differential memory effects for immediate and delayed feedback: a delta rule explanation of feedback timing efforts. Paper presented to the annual convention of the Association for Educational Communications and Technology, Houston, TX. [ERIC Document Reproduction Center ED 430 550.]

Clariana, R.B., and Lee, D. (2001). Recognition and recall tasks with feedback. *Educational technology research and development, 49* (3), 23-35.

Farquar, J.D., and Regian, J.W. (1994). The type and timing of feedback within an intelligent console-operations tutor. Paper presented at the 1994 Conference on Human Factors and Ergonomics Society.

Kern-Dunlap, L. (1992). Effects of a videotape feedback package on the peer interactions of children with serious behavioral and emotional challenges. *Journal of applied behavior analysis, 25* (2), 355-364.

Sasaki, Y. (1997). Individual variation in a Japanese sentence comprehension task—form, function, and strategies. *Applied linguistics, 19* (4), 508-537.

Van Geert, P. (1991). A dynamic systems model of cognitive and language growth. *Psychological review, 98* (1), 3-53.

Myth 10

Glenberg, A.M., Sanocki, T., Epstein, W., and Morris, C. (1987). Enhancing calibration of comprehension. *Journal of experimental psychology: general, 116* (2), 119-136.

Glenberg, A.M., Wilkinson, A.C., and Epstein, W. (1992). The illusion of knowing: failure in the self-assessment of comprehension. In T.O. Nelson, editor. *Metacognition: core readings.* Boston: Allyn & Bacon.

Olson, N. (2000). Realism of confidence in witness identification of faces and voices. (Unpublished doctoral dissertation.) Uppsala, Sweden: Uppsala University.

Schnackenberg, H.L., Sullivan, H.J., Leader, L.R., and Jones, E.E.K. (1998). Learner preferences and achievement under differing amounts of learner practice. *Educational technology research and development, 46,* 5-15.

Stone, N.J. (2000). Exploring the relationship between calibration and self-regulated learning. *Educational psychology review, 4,* 437-475.

Myth 11

Boulton, R.E.S., Libert, B.D., and Samek, S.M. (2000). *Cracking the value code: how successful businesses are creating wealth in the new economy.* New York: HarperBusiness/HarperCollins Publishers Inc., 17-19.

Myth 12

Van Buren, M.E., and Erskine, W. (2002). *State of the industry: ASTD's annual review of trends in employer-provided training in the United States.* Alexandria, VA: American Society for Training & Development.

About the Authors

Harold D. Stolovitch and **Erica J. Keeps** share a common passion—developing people. Together they have devoted a combined total of more than 70 years to make workplace learning and performance both enjoyable and effective. Their research and consulting activities have involved them in numerous projects with major corporations such as Hewlett-Packard, Sun Microsystems, Oracle, General Motors, Bell Canada, Telecom Asia, Canadian Pacific Railway, Alcan, Prudential, and Century 21. Their dedication to improving workplace learning and performance is reflected in the workshops they run internationally on training delivery, instructional design, and performance consulting. Stolovitch and Keeps are the principals of HSA Learning & Performance Solutions LLC, specialists in the application of instructional technology and human performance technology to business, industry, government, and the military. They are co-editors of both editions of the award-winning *Handbook of Human Performance Technology: A Comprehensive Guide for Analyzing and Solving Performance Problems in Organizations* and *Improving Individual and Organizational Performance Worldwide* published by Jossey-Bass/Pfeiffer. They are co-editors and co-authors of the Learning and Performance Toolkit series published Pfeiffer. Stolovitch and Keeps are also the authors of the award-winning best-seller *Telling Ain't Training,* published by ASTD Press.

Harold D. Stolovitch, CPT, is a graduate of both McGill University in Canada and Indiana University in the United States, where he completed a Ph.D. and post-doctoral work in instructional systems technology. With one foot solidly grounded in the academic world and the other in the workplace, Stolovitch has conducted a large number of research studies and practical projects always aimed at achieving high learning and performance results. In addition to creating countless instructional materials for a broad range of work settings, Stolovitch has authored almost 200 articles, research reports, book chapters, and books. He is a past president of the International Society for Performance Improvement (ISPI), former editor of the *Performance Improvement Journal,* and editorial board member of several human resource and performance technology journals. He has won numerous awards throughout his 43-year career including the Thomas F. Gilbert Award for Distinguished Professional Achievement, ISPI's highest honor; Member-for-Life of ISPI; and the Canadian Society for Training and Development's most prestigious President's Award for lifetime contribution to the field. Stolovitch is an emeritus professor, Université de Montréal, where he headed the instructional and performance technology programs, and a clinical professor of human performance at work, University of Southern California.

Erica J. Keeps, CPT, holds a master's degree in educational psychology from Wayne State University, Detroit, and a bachelor's degree from the University of Michigan, where she later became a faculty member in the Graduate Business School Executive Education Center. Her 33-year professional career has included training management positions with J. L. Hudson Co. and Allied Supermarkets and senior-level learning and performance consulting with a wide variety of organizations. Keeps has not only produced and supervised the production of numerous instructional materials and performance management systems, but has also published extensively on improving workplace learning and performance. She has provided staff development for instructional designers, training administrators, and performance engineers. Keeps has been acknowledged by many learning and performance leaders as a caring mentor and major influence in their careers. She is a former executive board member of the International Society for Performance Improvement, a past president of the Michigan Chapter of ISPI, and a Member-for-Life of both the Michigan and Montreal ISPI chapters. Her many awards for outstanding contributions to instructional and performance technology include ISPI's Distinguished Service Award for leadership.

The authors reside in Los Angeles and can be reached through their Website: www.hsa-lps.com.